Muder for Lust

To connect with the author, please visit
www.robertsteadman.net.

Published by
TRIAL JUSTICE PUBLICATIONS

ISBN: 979-8-8692-5837-3

Printed in the United States of America

A COMMUNITY LEADER'S MURDEROUS,
OBSESSION DRIVEN PLAN TO POSSESS
ANOTHER MAN'S WIFE

Murder for Lust

ROBERT A. STEADMAN

TRIAL JUSTICE PUBLICATIONS

Praise for *Murder for Lust*

In *Murder for Lust*, Steadman has crafted the perfect plot and reveals it in a special voice that makes it all believable. He introduces one twist after another and ties it together neatly to serve up a wonderful work sure to please and intrigue crime aficionados. In *Murder for Lust*, Steadman has created a masterful scenario in Traverse City, MI, sprinkled it with extraordinary characters that squirm, stumble and shine throughout. He writes of the incredible events and twists as if they were based on a true crime -- authoritative, level-headed, straightforward, not too emotional, like a reporter sharing the facts. . . . .

Steadman's expertise as a trial attorney adds authenticity to the story, which again reinforces the belief that people are so capable of acting in strange ways when it comes to matters of the heart and the heartless.

  — BookTrib

Like fine wine, writer Robert Steadman, an outstanding trial lawyer for sixty years, improves with each book. The authenticity is unquestionable. His first, *I Killed Sam*, chronicled his defense of a battered woman in 1956 who killed her brutal husband and faced discriminatory laws that appeared to guarantee imprisonment for life. He followed with *The "Hog Wild" War*, the story of his remarkable, International Law changing, 1959 representation of a small, hog farmer against the billionaire feed corporation that took advantage of him. This, his third book, *Murder for Lust*, is an electrifying crime thriller set in his hometown of Traverse City, MI. His plot grabs your attention, with unbridled, obsessive lust that leads to fraud, financial ruin, and death. A great read for crime buffs, once started it is impossible to put down. The plot, the characters and the court trial action would make an incredible movie.

  — Pamela Wakefield, Shelter Advocate for Traverse City Women's Resource Center

Robert A. Steadman's *Murder for Lust* opens with the jubilant union of Jimmy Jones and the beguilingly beautiful Alice Bramer, and becomes a pulse-pounding, beautifully written thriller with characters that feel real. The writing shines through the pages and Steadman has the uncanny ability for crafting dramatic scenes and infusing the writing with realism. Reading this book felt like watching a movie — the scenes are vivid, the characters are believable, and the plot offers suspenseful moments that keep readers racing through the pages. . . . . .

Readers will hate the villain and deeply sympathize with Alice's defiant defense. Steadman masterfully weaves a complex tale of financial fraud, dubious land deals, and murder-for-hire, creating a web of suspense that is absorbing. The psychological depth of the narrative adds an extra layer of tension as readers are taken into the mind of Dex Henderson, exploring the dark corners of obsession. The characters' moral dilemmas and internal struggles contribute to the story's depth, making it more than just a suspenseful thriller.

—The Book Commentary

Steadman is a master storyteller with a knack for creating relatable and lovable characters, drawing readers into their world with ease. Jimmy and Alice's love is beautifully depicted, making their plight all the more heartbreaking when tragedy strikes. Dex's villainy dominates the narrative and readers will want to follow his every step. His inner world is finely drawn and the author uses his machinations to create layers of suspense and tension in the narrative. What sets *Murder for Lust* apart is Steadman›s ability to weave a complex tale of financial fraud, dubious land deals, and murder-for-hire into an absorbing narrative. Each chapter unveils new layers of deception and intrigue, keeping readers on the edge of their seats until the very end.

—The Book Commentary

I dedicate this book to the three most
accomplished and intelligent women I have
known and loved unconditionally.

Bernice Trimble Steadman,
my wife

Calista Steadman Schwartz,
my sister

Calista Anne Steadman,
my mother

Table of Contents

Alice 1

Dex 5

The Plan 10

Jane 14

The Subdivision 20

Jimmy.. 25

Guarantee 29

Ben... 35

The New Alice.. 40

Joe Binds... 50

Joe Reports 52

Lawsuit.. 55

Response 59

Preliminary Motion 64

Perjury 78

2nd Investigation 81

New Report 87

Timetable Adjustment 89

Trial Preparation 91

Love 94

Attack 99

Again.. 108

Counter Plan 112

Trial 120

Opening 122

Plaintiffs' Case 127

Handwriting... 145

Dex Direct 159

Cross Examination 161

Final Arguments 177

Verdict 186

Finish 189

Alice

Alice Bramer walked sedately to the altar to marry Jimmy Jones. It was one of those lovely days in June that Michigan's Traverse City celebrates in its relatively short summer, when the cool, northerly breezes from the East and West Bays keep the temperature at a perfect, seventies' level. That was all well and good until Alice stood by the groom and her father removed her veil. There was an involuntary, group gasp at the beauty of the bride. Dressed in a lovely, traditionally cut, white wedding gown and tall enough to stand eye to eye with Jimmy's six feet in her low heels, her flaming red hair and fine features dominated the scene. The temperature became almost unbearably warm for most of the male guests. Heat radiated from her without any coquettish posturing on her part.

Jimmy, decked out in his tuxedo, was a dashing figure quite at odds with his normal, small-town look. His friends from the morning coffee group at the Park Place had been dubious when Jimmy told them that he met her in Ann Arbor while on vacation and proudly claimed the attraction had been shared and immediate. Jimmy didn't impress as a major hunk although a good-looking man, and the idea that any woman would be immediately attracted, particularly in a sexual manner, was difficult to process.

The feeling was magnified by the fact that he admitted to being ten years older than her.

Jimmy had been so over the top talking about her as an amazing athlete, a brain working in marketing for a major firm and blindingly gorgeous, that they had lower expectations with each additional superlative. He was obviously a goner. They finally just cut him some slack and privately joked about his teenage crush. He was constantly making sure he let his coffee group friends know how he had pursued and managed to convince her to marry him in less than six months. Before the scheduled ceremony he had been going around with the biggest grin they had ever seen. They didn't realize he was looking forward to their sudden awakening to her looks when she appeared for the first time in Traverse City. Jimmy was smart enough to know he had been extolling her virtues far too often and in such unbelievable terms that his friends were certain he was overselling his bride to be. Knowing what a tremendous shock it was going to be, he had gleefully invited all ten of his coffee group friends, including the wives of the married ones, to the wedding and reception. He was looking forward to blowing their minds with his bride and had difficulty waiting at the altar for her to appear. The first view of her flaming red hair cut below her shoulders, gorgeous features, and tall, exceptionally beautiful body, did all that Jimmy had expected. She was incredibly spectacular, and he was confident all ten of the coffee group, regardless of their age, were dazzled. He was right on with his plan. Their reactions were along the lines of, "My God, he wasn't overselling her," and "What a knockout!"

The wives knew their husbands were making the inevitable comparisons. They were not happy since most were past the point where they believed they could compete with youth, and it was even harder when the girl was blessed with great looks and a body to match. Now that they all had the opportunity to see her, the biggest question going the rounds was how in hell Jimmy had managed to get her to accept his proposal. Well-liked and respected for his business acumen, there was no way they could imagine him measuring up to that youthful, incredible bride. The consensus was that there was no reasonable answer other than huge luck.

Ben Bradshaw, Jimmy's best friend and attorney, knew better than the other coffee group members what an outstanding man Jimmy was, a solid family man and, smart as hell. The kind of man a mature, thinking woman would be drawn to. Ben's estimate of Alice, drawn from his relatively short time talking with her, was that she was that kind of woman. That didn't stop him from kidding Jimmy about his luck. He took the next time he was alone for a moment with Jimmy to congratulate him.

"You're the luckiest guy known to man in getting a young woman like Alice to marry you. She's everything you told us and lots more. Excellent job, buddy, you weren't overselling the bride you won. I can see how much she loves you and you deserve it. Her family is great too. You will never have a problem with your in-laws. They are all genuinely warm and loving. They remind me of my own family."

Jimmy was thrilled at Ben's accolades, and they sat aside from the others for a time as Jimmy shared more about Alice's background. Ben was in awe of how his friend had accomplished his courtship and was almost in a daze at her beauty and apparent athleticism. She stood so tall while moving so gracefully. He knew Jimmy was giving him the straight dope.

His companions were in full conversational mode; having a ball talking about how beautiful and vibrant she was.

The general feeling was that Jimmy was on top of the world with his gorgeous, young bride.

Ben's comments were true to a fault about her family. They were down to earth folks who obviously doted on Alice. He spent some time with them and could see the apple had dropped from them both. Her mother was bright and open in her conversation and Alice's father came across the same. She reminded Ben of his own mother. His was a close-knit family and it was clear Alice had the same support. When she walked down the aisle on her father's arm, he left the entire group of spectators pleased with his athletic stature and his approving smile. He was tall and she matched his height in her heels. He gave her away with a flourish and obvious happiness for her. Her younger sister Lena was her bridesmaid and when together, they were great to look at. They were a hit with all of Jimmy's friends and the wedding was a celebration for his new, extended family.

There was no question in Ben's mind that Alice and Jimmy were very much in love. Their passion was evident, and it carried over in their life together. Ben visited their home often and was pleased by their luck in finding each other. She was dramatically intelligent and had become Jimmy's full partner in the planning and development of his projects. Her sense of humor was terrific and occasionally bawdy enough to keep Jimmy in an almost perpetual smile. The old, reserved, workaholic Jimmy was gone, and the new edition was fun to be around. What they obviously shared led Ben to seriously consider looking harder for a woman to enhance his own life although he had yet to meet the "one" for him.

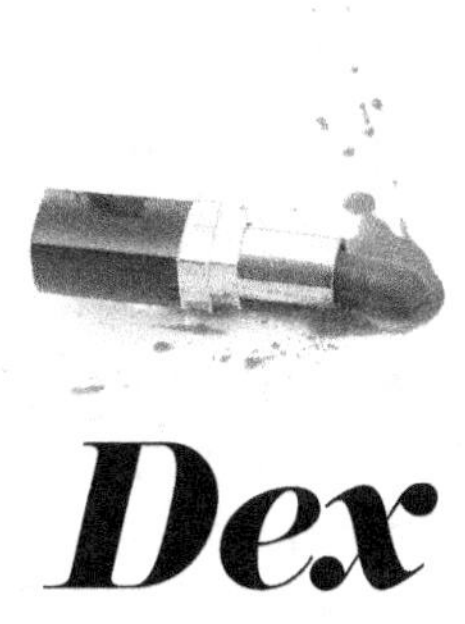

Dex

Dex **Henderson had** been standing with the coffee regulars when they saw Alice for the first time and was astounded by Jimmy's good fortune in finding and landing such a beautiful woman for his bride. Dex had never seen such a gorgeous woman and stood next to Ben for a time at the reception saying little and attempting unsuccessfully to hide the depth of his reaction. He was monumentally lustful for her and could feel the desire building in him. Ben noticed the evident change in Dex's demeanor but assumed it was the same manifestation of surprise the entire coffee group was feeling. He put it away in his memory Bank without a second thought.

Dex took the opportunity to talk with Alice for quite a long time at the reception, intending to give her a first impression of his impressive, (to him), stature in the community. He bragged about his work as president at the Bank and mentioned in passing his establishment of the Bank's foundation fund to help the employees. She was interested in that approach and conceded she had never heard of such a marvelous program for a work force. He told her how he had supported Jimmy's land developments by financing them as the man in charge of financing such projects at the Bank and how much he admired Jimmy's capabilities in the area. She beamed at his praise for Jimmy and was very favorably impressed with his friendly manner and his obvious, long term, strong financial support of his work.

He came away from his extended conversation with his almost uncontrollable reaction to her beauty intact while making a mental comparison between him and Jimmy. Jimmy was the clear loser. Dex knew from his first sight of her, buttressed by their conversation, that she was his woman, and Jimmy was just an inconvenience in the way of his conquest. He dismissed Jimmy as an inconsequential barrier at best. He had known for years that a special woman would finally come along to satisfy his belief in his extraordinary genius and ultimate desirability to women. That day had finally come, and his mind was racing with the new possibilities. He attempted to make sure no one had a clue as to how tremendous her effect on him had been but had no idea that the intense nature of his attention to her had caught Ben's eye. He was confident his feelings were his own and would have dismissed Ben's reaction as unimportant at best if he had realized his reaction was observed.

He was Jimmy's banker and three years older than him at thirty-eight. As president of the local Bank, he had been instrumental in providing Jimmy with the open-ended line of credit that had supported Jimmy's remarkable success as a land developer over the past seven years. The Bank had made substantial profits from Jimmy's developments and Dex received a great deal of credit from his superiors at the main offices of the Bank for his decision to back Jimmy, a young entrepreneur who had started his business with a small inheritance and never stopped working hard and making substantial profits. Dex knew the opportunity for sharing in Jimmy's profits would come along and was confident he could manipulate Jimmy well enough to take a worthwhile share. It would be lucrative indeed. Furnishing the money had given him substantial influence in Jimmy's planned developments under the guise of concern for the Bank's investment and he had learned all facets of Jimmy's deals. Before Alice, his only interest in Jimmy had been future theft of money but that all changed at the wedding.

He left the reception early with a building sense of anger that Jimmy had found the woman he felt entitled to own. His obsession since his teen years had been to possess in the biblical sense, a beautiful, ravishing woman as his mate; one so outstanding that she would present his lofty personal standards of public position and power to the world. For his purposes, all she needed was looks and a body he could enjoy. He did not concern himself with her intelligence since his well-hidden secret was his belief that he had an incredible, out of this world intellect, along with remarkable irresistibility for any woman he chose. He reveled in his sense of power over the rest of the public he believed so universally dull and had no question in his mind but that he was vastly more intelligent than any woman he determined would be his wife. His demands would be youth, beauty, and sex. He chuckled as he assumed his litany of demands would be slavishly catered to by his wife, and he would receive his due through the thrill of unlimited, deviant sex and from dominating her as the superior being he believed he was.

He thought whatever woman he chose would be so thankful and smitten with him that he would have all of that and more. He had always believed that, when he found the ideal woman, he dreamed of, she would find him irresistible and would fall deeply in love with him. She would want to perform whatever sexual fantasy he wanted. He had satisfied his sexual life exclusively with prostitutes who performed his fantasies for his money and were compliant on demand. Alice was the first woman he had ever considered for a wife, and he determined he would do whatever was required to have her serving his, and only his, needs.

During his tenure as president of the Bank branch in Traverse City, he had continued to hide his belief in his extraordinary intellect since he thought it would cause negative feelings in the Bank staff and potentially impede his ability to conduct his criminal activities. He was engaged in a series of scams involving skimming funds from depositors' accounts. He had developed the ability to forge signatures through techniques learned from books. With practice he had become particularly good at it and, because he limited his depredation amounts, had been successful over the years. His scams were his monetary bread and butter. He was riding high and tremendously proud of himself. He kept his salary and checks for living costs in an account in his Bank. He kept his scam money in a Bank account under an assumed name in southern Michigan.

He had adopted a pleasant, friendly manner, easily acting as a nice guy. The community leaders and coffee mates he dealt with every day were impressed while he hid his laughter at how dull they all were. He sat with them without sharing much but always maintaining his "good friend" identity. He also made sure he came across as a benevolent boss at the Bank where he addressed each employee's particular needs for birthdays, problems with children and vacations. He had set up the fund that provided preschool help for their children and little acts of kindness like paying for babysitting and an occasional dinner out as rewards for excellence while privately reviling their stupidity and trust.

He fostered a persona as an easy mark who could always be counted on for help. His "friends" in the coffee group were always welcome at the Bank and quick personal loans were available for all of them. Whether they used his assistance or not, they all understood he was ready to help and counted him as a friend indeed. It was so easy for him to manipulate everyone that his arrogance had grown beyond his early dreams of power and dominance. He thought often about his incredible abilities and saw the world as his to roam and rape.

He was doing very well as a thief, having amassed a hidden nest egg of a half-million dollars in his downstate account. His success in accumulating so much money from his scams was additional proof to him of how extraordinary he was. The Bank employees had no idea of his contempt for them and had failed to suspect his frauds. He believed his father's nepotism in awarding him the Presidency of the Third Michigan Bank and Trust branch office in Traverse City was recognition of his superior intellect. He hid his contempt and anger for his father, having always resented that he had spent so little time with him while growing up.

Having been given the position of leadership in Traverse City, he had taken advantage of it fully. He had started with the old maxim of "a little here, a little there" but had graduated to bigger amounts as his success fed his feelings of invincibility and power. He never thought of his actions as criminal, enjoying the largesse he took from the fools who surrounded him. He congratulated himself for winning the game, day by day. Any pain or harm he caused met the same lack of concern. He thought only of himself and, as far as injury to anyone scammed or affected by a loss, he didn't give a damn. It had become fun for him, and he thought of his victims as bugs, pinned to the wall. Alice would be fun of a different kind. The sex would be wonderfully perverse with moves he salivated about.

The Plan

He realized that he had provided Jimmy with the means to woo and win the gorgeous Alice, the woman he now viewed as his rightful possession. His loans had insured substantial profits for Jimmy from his subdivision developments, making him quite well off. Jimmy often thanked him for his assistance and Dex had enjoyed it for years. Now, realizing that his help had given Jimmy the means and time to court Alice, he regretted that support. During the next week, Dex began to see the outline of a plan to rectify the cruel mistake of her marriage to someone else.

He opened his bedroom closet door and looked into the mirror hanging there. He thought the image of the thirty-eight-year-old man who looked back at him was handsome and still youthful. He saw a rugged cowboy. His pot belly was belted in with an exceptionally large, ostentatious, western-style buckle and the little stoop from his now-and-then back twinges was hardly notice-able to anyone else. It was certainly not a detriment to him in his inflated view of himself. He was proud he was six feet tall and that his hair was still abundant although beginning to thin a bit. He had always believed it was one of his best features and thought of it as an especially attractive brown. He paid his barber lavishly to keep it precisely cut with long, western style sideburns like those of the heroes of the western movies he loved.

Traverse City had a small town's informal view of fashion, but he challenged it with his custom-sewn, snapped shirts; cowboy-inspired, black, pressed, designer jeans; and very ornate snakeskin and crocodile boots. They were handmade for him with a wonderful fit for his small feet and he had several pairs featuring unusual colors and skin types, all with a price tag reaching more than six hundred a pair. Although he did not wear a holster and gun, he imagined himself as one of those premier, legendary gunmen of the old, wild west. He had come to call himself "Tex" in private and occasionally slapped his hand down to the mythical holster to pull his gun. It was Tex who stared back at him from the mirror with approval. He knew his coffee-group friends were amused by his clothing affectations, but he relied on his willingness to dress differently from the crowd as a means of standing out and earning recognition as an important leader in the community. He gloried in his western outfits, knowing they set him apart without any words needed. Another testament to his innate superiority.

If there was an unusual feature in the reflected image, it was the eyebrow elevated above his right eye. He believed it made him even more handsome in a tough sort of way. He had thought, as a teen, it had the appearance of a battle scar or a blow from a fight and that girls would be attracted to him for it. It had become such a part of him he no longer thought about it. He knew there were few men without some identifying feature and had always believed his was interesting and gave him a mystery face for bamboozling the girls. After high school he had graduated from the callow girls and had relied on hookers to please him.

They accepted his bouts of sexual cruelty and deviance so long as his money held out.

"Alice will want me as much or more than I want her," he told the mirror, and smiled in satisfaction. He had played "mirror, mirror on the wall" for most of his teen years, buttressing his love affair with himself. He finished his gaze into the mirror with, "Wait till Alice really sees me as I am. She is going to provide everything I want and love doing it. She won't be willing to wait, night after night." As that picture of her, naked and beckoning to him filled his mind, his physical reaction was intense. He knew she would be so much more exciting than any of his many prostitutes. To top it off, she would be available anytime he wanted and as long as he wanted her. It pleased him to think that she would be worth something when he had finished with her. With what he would teach her, he would be able to find work for her as a whore for a few years after he was done with her. Acting as her pimp would be a new venture although he thought gleefully there would be little left to sell.

Although his belief in his own brilliance would have been a joke at best if known by his friends, he had a slyness and craftiness that kept him going successfully. He knew he needed to eliminate Jimmy. But taking Jimmy out of the equation would be only a first step if Alice was left with independent means. There had to be a real opportunity for showing his support and affection for her and, if she was financially ruined, he would be the logical man to step in to help. She would be vulnerable to his desirability and desperately in need of financial and grief-easing help.

It became obvious to him that Jimmy would have to be eliminated sooner rather than later or the time for eventual success would take too long. He wanted her sooner, not later. He assumed she would appreciate a slow initial approach although he knew she would come to love and want him quickly once Jimmy was no longer in the picture. There was simply no way she would be uninterested in his attentions. He had so much to offer her he reasoned it would be a relatively brief period of time before she came to him in the biblical sense he dreamed of. A subservient wife who accepted his position as the head of the household entitled to demand sexual obedience and expecting to suffer and accept punishment with or without cause as evidence of his dominance. His mind had continued to paint a picture of a naked Alice, and his desire for her was so strong he could not control his body's reaction. That first time with her would be proof of his superiority and her compliant, loving subjugation, the final victory in his plan.

Jane

Thinking about ways to involve Jimmy in debt, Jane Bishop popped into his mind. She was a very wealthy woman in her nineties who, due to her failing cognitive abilities, he had been scamming for a year with checks he had made out for her to a fictitious company he had formed in southern Michigan. His thefts from her had already amounted to more than $150,000. While engineering the thefts from her substantial Bank account, he had hungrily eyed her seventy-five-acre property on the west boundary of Traverse City. It was a level area on the hillside slopes with maples and oaks in an extensive wooded area that would provide trees for a subdivision as well as a nice park area for community use. The site had lain fallow for years and had a large amount of fertile soil for grass lawns and flower beds along with magnificent views of the city and both bays from its perch above the city.

It had been appraised at $3,000,000 when an offer was made to purchase it for development. She had refused that offer or even to consider any other offers. It had been her husband's and her home for more than sixty years. Her children had spent many happy years there and the home was substantial enough to be called a mansion. She loved her home and acreage with its glorious views, but, since turning down the offer, her mind had quickly yielded to major loss of cognitive ability.

Dex had been the only representative of the Bank who had met with her in the past year, and he could see a beautiful attack on Jimmy and Alice's financial position if the Bank could take Jane's seventy-five acres. It was prime development land and Jimmy was a leading developer. He was sure Jimmy would jump at the chance to own and develop such an incredible parcel and thought offering the land to Jimmy at a low price would set his plan for Alice in motion. He had already given Jimmy a substantial line of credit and it had been paid off promptly. Jimmy's dealings with Dex at the Bank had been profitable for both parties and Dex thought he could bring the Bank along on enough financing for a new project to put Jimmy and Alice in an extreme position of debt. Having the ability to guarantee full financial support of Jimmy's development with a new mortgage would be the final inducement.

He knew he needed to encumber Jane's land heavily to prevent her children from having the ability to fight foreclosure. To make his plan work he prepared a mortgage in her name in the amount of $900,000 along with a check made out to Ohio Home Construction, a new company he would form with a DBA in Ohio. He had practiced assiduously forging her signature and was able to do the forgery easily and so well it had passed muster in the Bank for more than a year. His scamming had already reduced her balance to about $100,000 from its usual $250,000, leaving sufficient funds to cash the check to his new, Ohio company after approval of her mortgage and deposit of the mortgage funds in her account. The check would leave her estate with no ability to manage payment of the new mortgage and he would then foreclose.

The Bank would own her land when the foreclosure was completed. He was looking at less than a year for the foreclosure to be completed and another six months for Jimmy to have invested sufficiently in development to make repayment impossible if Jimmy was out of the picture. He would be able to ensure Alice was penniless and homeless. With his plan carried out, she would be desperately in need of his support and care. He felt like a teen again. "Boy," he thought, "this is going to be everything I have ever wanted, in spades. No more prostitutes and big cash payments for sex."

He had a banking meeting scheduled in Toledo in a few weeks, and planned carefully how he would set the scam up in Ohio without exposure. He needed to establish a construction company with a DBA in the name of Otto Cambridge, the name he had selected for the owner of the Ohio construction company he would report to his Bank board as supposedly collaborating with Jane. He considered his plan foolproof and easy to accomplish with a little time in Ohio.

He had carefully accumulated the items he needed for his disguise, buying them in communities away from town where he was unknown. Each purchase had been so insignificant it was never notable enough for the salesclerk to even look at him when he put it on the counter. The makeup kit he bought had been a Halloween special with several beards of different lengths and colors while the shade darkening ability was quite common but would be enough to change his looks. He was ready.

He thought Otto Cambridge would look quite dashing in a beard. It would provide a new persona without the slightest indication of what Dex looked like. He thought, in passing, how Alice would react to his beard. She would be thrilled, he was sure. "I'll grow one for her," he reflected, and it gave him additional pleasure. "Damn," he thought, "who but me could plan this out and make it happen so perfectly? I am going to have Alice and a nice big payday at the same time."

He finished his banking meeting in Toledo and waved goodbye with a smile as he gave the impression of starting home. Working quickly, he assumed the fake beard and new glasses and then drove to the court building in Concord County where he approached the clerk and asked for a DBA form. She was quite pleasant, and he was working on the form within a few minutes. He prepared and signed the DBA in the name of Ohio Home Construction. He assigned an address he had found for a vacant lot in Concordia, and filed under the owner's name of Otto Cambridge, paying cash for the transaction. The check he had prepared over Jane's forged signature was to the new company, Ohio Home Construction, in the amount of $950,000 and he knew he would have no difficulty approving its cashing since her signature would appear to be genuine and he could indicate her supposed conversations with him about building homes on her property for her children.

It was certain the loss of so much of Jane's money would be investigated and eventually listed as a major scam when Ohio Home Construction was found to be a unit without substance located on a vacant lot in Concordia, Ohio. But with no identification of the scammer, it would be put on the ever-expanding list of scams against the elderly unable to be solved or resolved. He thought the local Ohio police would gnash their teeth at the absence of clues and it gave him another moment of self-praise for his brilliance. He had already reduced her Bank account balance to $100,000.00. With the check to Ohio Home Construction that included another fifty thousand dollars over the mortgage money, there would be hardly anything left in her account. There would be much too little money left to support litigation by her children attempting to prevent foreclosure of the mortgage he had forged and filed. He was sure no attorney in Traverse City would challenge the bank on a foreclosure. His plan was moving forward inexorably.

He knew he needed Jane to die immediately in an undetectable way and went online to study lethal agents. Abrin looked like the best bet since it was colorless and quick. He needed something that would mimic death from old age when her body was found. He had checked her nursing schedule and noted that her nurse was going to be gone the afternoon of Wednesday next week and he planned a meeting with Jane on that day.

Since Abrin was a poison that had several medical uses in minute amounts, he theorized it would be found in most drugstores. He decided to burglarize one. He had spent time in Concordia looking for an address for his fake company and knew the town well. It was of medium size, with about thirty thousand residents and he settled on the main drugstore. His late at night break-in was simple enough. The broken glass at his proposed entry point caused no visible alarm. He waited half an hour and then entered. He found a small bottle of Abrin in the cabinet labeled "Danger" and, once again, was thrilled at his ability and success. His plan was moving smoothly.

He came to Jane's home in the afternoon after the nurse's regular morning time. She was napping as he entered her room and woke slowly. She had been resting comfortably and he moved slowly to not disturb her as he carefully planted a folder of home designs and forged correspondence with Otto Cambridge, the owner of Ohio

Home Construction. Having stashed the proof of her ability to contract and sign documents along with the evidence of her planning the homes for her kids, he dropped some Abrin in a glass of water and helped her drink it. She died in pain, choking, helpless, and alone except for her murderer. He rinsed the glass and replaced it on her side table so there was no evidence of her having had a drink, something he knew she was incapable of. Her pain and death were inconsequential to him. He was proud of his simple, effective finish of Jane Bishop's life. They should thank me for ending her useless life, he thought, but knew the fools never would since no one would ever know he had killed her.

The Subdivision

Dex's **forged Bishop** mortgage for $900,000 went through without question when he described her signing it and her purpose for the money. His forgery perfectly matched her signature on documents in her file over the past five years. When the loan review board questioned the large amount, he indicated she had decided to build homes on her land for her children and had quotes for completion of her plans requiring the bulk of the mortgage amount. He discussed her plan to pay off the mortgage from the proceeds of her projected sale of land not needed for the houses. The value of the unattached land was around two million and the board was satisfied. When the check to Ohio Home Construction went through, his scam was complete, and it was a simple matter to run the check through the Bank account he had established in Ohio for the fake company. He had the cash in his possession within a week and made sure Otto Cambridge became a disappearing ghost.

As he had planned, Jane's children found her estate so depleted they could not pay or fight. Although it took a few months, the foreclosure was eventually complete, and the

Bank now owned Jane's seventy-five acres and home. Dex was confident he could talk Jimmy into a deal that would set up his opportunity to destroy Jimmy's and Alice's financial position.

Dex called Jimmy with the news that the Bank now owned the finest parcel in the Traverse City area for development and he was able to sell it to Jimmy for $1,900,000, a figure more than a million dollars less that the earlier appraisal but which secured and cleared the Bank's expenditures with a profit of at least one million dollars. It was a legitimate offer and Jimmy was intrigued.

To Dex's complete surprise, Jimmy and Alice declined because the major investment required was larger than they were willing to mortgage. Jimmy had paid off the line of credit used before and thought the anticipated new debt would be too large. Alice agreed. To their immense surprise, Dex offered to expand the line of credit without a top limit for the express purpose of developing the land in question. Jimmy was incredulous.

"Do you mean you will get the Bank to come up with the massive costs of putting roads and water into the parcel? It will be almost a year in development before we can market lots and the interest on that size mortgage will be a much too costly addition to our overall costs. We must assume such a mortgage will require additional collateral and we are not going to include our home in any deal. It is paid off and we intend living there for many years."

Dex said, "This is based on our years of friendship. I will give you our minimum interest rate of four percent and will personally guarantee you are not harmed in any way including any proposed loss of your home. Obviously, you need more collateral than the speculative value of the development and, unfortunately, the home will need to be included in the collateral. It is worth more than a quarter of a million and it will increase the collateral. I need to include it to satisfy the Bank board's position in granting the mortgage."

Jimmy adamantly balked at including their home, but Dex again stated his personal guarantee their home would not be included in the unlikely event the mortgage was foreclosed and there was no way they would be harmed. Jimmy and Alice discussed it into the night but, finally, the potential profits in the range of eight million dollars from developing the property would be financial security for years and Dex's guarantee was the final ingredient that convinced them they should sign the new mortgage. Dex had been a good friend and had led the Bank in its endorsement and participation in financing Jimmy's growth as the leading developer in the city. Jimmy valued his friendship and could see that he was looking out for them with his offer to fund the subdivision they would design and build.

Alice voted yes and Jimmy agreed. Dex was pleased but not surprised. He had assumed they would jump at the Bank's offer, and he had won them over with his guarantee. He chuckled at the ease with which he was moving forward with his plan. Jimmy was going to be toast and the beautiful Alice would be in his home soon enough. He had the mortgage document ready in a day and the three of them met in his office to sign it.

Dex signed for the Bank and said, "You won't regret this day. I am looking forward to walking the streets of a fantastic subdivision located on one of the most beautiful spots in the Traverse City area. I am confident your profits from this deal alone, will be more than you have earned from any of your prior, completed developments."

Jimmy answered. "We will owe you our gratitude when

this is done, and you walk those streets as you say. We both believe in the site and what we can do with it. Alice has become my business partner with a knack for numbers superior to mine and her analysis projects substantial profits well in excess of your assumptions. We thank you for your friendship and financial support."

When they had left his office, Dex leaned back in his expensive leather chair and daydreamed about what he would have her do. Her willing participation was a given once he had shown her his superiority and his immense desirability had taken hold. He thought his plan had been fun from the beginning and his self-approval was in full force. Money and sex with Alice were his goals and their place in his future was now assured. It was hard to stay quiet, but he managed.

After signing the new mortgage, Jimmy and Alice set out to develop Traverse City's finest subdivision on what had been Jane Bishop's land. It really was a beautiful site, and they could see the massive potential profits. Their final subdivision design gave them 126 lots with a minimum lot value of $150,000 each. The views of the bay and the city were breathtaking, and builders were already clamoring for lots. The subdivision was going to be ready for lot sales when the water system was completed. They already had the roads in, and water line installation scheduled, having taken full advantage of the summer months. The total bid for both services had been a little less than $3,000,000 and the subdivision was moving forward to completion with exceptional speed. With the purchase price for the land, the total Bank mortgage was going to be almost five million dollars and the lot sales would be at least thirteen million or more. They expected low additional costs for incidentals and marketing. Jimmy

and Alice were working together on the marketing cam-
paign that would begin in the winter and the project was
so outstanding they could count on the profits coming.
Alice had become Jimmy's most trusted assistant with her
strong intelligence and drive. Every question about the
future of the company had become a joint decision. Their
working together had strengthened their love and Alice
had come to love Traverse City as her home as well. They
shared a deep appreciation of all they had accomplished
in the relatively short period of their marriage and the
future looked great indeed. She wanted a family and their
plans for children were on hold for a brief time only.

Jimmy

Watching their progress, Dex was jubilant. The sub-division was near completion and Jimmy was set up for the massive failure Dex had planned. All he needed was to take Jimmy out of the picture as soon as possible. Although bringing anyone else into any part of the plan was dangerous, he thought doing the job himself was too risky. If he was identified as involved in any way in Jimmy's death it would potentially lead to a devastating criminal prosecution. He needed to hire a killer for Jimmy.

He had researched the online references for "adventurers" which he believed was a code word for people willing to do hits for money. He had accumulated several mobile phone burners as a means of hiding his identity and had called two numbers without luck. On the third call he found what he was looking for. A man who seemed as careful as he was. He had a short conversation with a man who called himself "Ray" who told him, "Call me again in a day at this number if you are still interested in talking more but only call if you have business to discuss."

Dex called Ray the next day. Ray asked specifically, "Do you have sufficient funds to handle my fees for work, assuming they will be substantial?" Dex carefully answered, "I can handle them for the work I want done." Several calls later they had established an agreement to kill Jimmy. The twenty thousand dollars in cash demanded was more than he had expected but Ray had indicated "that Dex's requirement that the death had to appear accidental added to the costs."

Ray gave specific instructions on the money drop. It became obvious he had been to Traverse City more than once when he told Dex "He wanted the drop made in the Park Place Hotel coffee shop, a place always busy and easy to access from the lobby." He directed Dex "to put the money envelope on the little side table about three feet left of the door as one entered." He said "there were always hats and other material there and that the envelope should be brown with a metal clasp, marked with the simple name, SAM." Dex should get a cup of coffee there on Thursday, two days after the call. To place the envelope on the table when he went into the coffee shop at 9."

Dex was impressed with what he perceived as a professional approach and, on Thursday, followed the directions to the letter. He came into the shop after the usual coffee group had broken up. His ten-thousand dollar down payment was left at the drop site, with the balance to be paid on success.

It never crossed his supposedly brilliant mind that he would be exposed to the killer the moment he left the envelope where directed. Ray was sitting in the coffee shop at a table where he could observe the drop and snapped a picture of Dex as it was made. He never took on a hit without some insurance and knowing his employer's identity was standard practice on his part. He picked up his envelope on the way out the door and followed Dex to the Bank. He noted Dex parked in the space marked President and, with little effort, compared his phone photo with a Bank promo document featuring Dex Henderson as President.

There was no doubt Henderson was his employer. A Bank president, no less.

He felt safe proceeding with the hit since there was no way a Bank president was going to betray him. It was a concern he faced with each job, and he needed to know he was covered against disclosure by his employer. He had the beginnings of a plan working in his mind and headed for Jimmy's office for surveillance. He needed to know when Jimmy left for home and what his route was. He followed Jimmy for several days before his plan matured. Ray was an experienced and resourceful, professional hitman. While viewing Jimmy's route home he had found just what he needed on a section of road with a sharp curve, a steep embankment just off the main road, and not much by way of guardrail or traffic. He had studied Jimmy's time from his office to his home and planned his attack for Jimmy's usual six o'clock travel on that roadway. The road would almost certainly be deserted at that time. He noted that Alice was working at home and Jimmy was always punctual in arriving for their cocktails and dinner.

When he saw Jimmy leave his office on the day he had picked, he immediately drove to his planned spot and parked beside the road with his emergency lights flashing. Sure enough, Jimmy almost immediately came around the curve. He saw the flashing lights and a man standing behind his car and waving his arms to stop. Ray had made it obvious he was in trouble and Jimmy stopped to help. As he moved from his car Ray approached and Jimmy found himself facing a gun and a man demanding his car.

"I see you left it running. All I want is your car," he said. "I don't want any of your personal stuff so you can get in and grab it, but quickly." Jimmy slid into the driver's seat and, as he turned to reach for his jacket and wallet, Ray viciously slugged him on the back of his head. When certain that Jimmy was unconscious from the blow he worked fast, turning Jimmy's car front wheels so that they veered over the side of the road. Using a four-foot rod he had carried behind him as he approached, Ray depressed the gas pedal to the highest rpm so that the car would smash through the guardrail and down the embankment. Jimmy, without his seat belt secured, plunged over two hundred feet to his death in a terrible crash on the rocks below. Thrown from the car at impact, his death was instantaneous.

Ray had driven out of sight before the next car came along. It had been perfectly planned and executed. His luck had held with no cars coming when he sent the car over the cliff. Ray was pleased at how easy it had been and looked forward to his next payment. His balance of ten thousand dollars was in an envelope on the table after his call confirming the kill. A nice piece of business, Ray thought, with a strong probability of eventual blackmail and many more dollars. Contrary to Dex's delusion, Ray knew how foolish the neophyte had been for trusting a stranger in a murder plot and making no discernible effort to hide his identity. Hardly up to par for a Bank president but Ray cut him a little slack for his presumedly, first-time murder. It made the eventual blackmail even more enticing, and Ray looked forward to fleecing the arrogant ass who had hired him. He regretted a bit his working for such small money for a bastard like Dex. Killing innocent women or children wasn't his thing and he would refuse any such killing unless they were witnesses who could identify him. First and foremost, he protected himself any anyone who might be a witness would be disposed of regardless of sex or age.

Guarantee

Jimmy's death was devastating to Alice. She was grief stricken and unable to plan or work on the subdivision through the funeral. The ceremony was beautiful, and it seemed like the whole town turned out to support her and say their final goodbyes to Jimmy. With less than two years between her wedding ceremony and this service of grief it was extraordinarily difficult for her to manage although she appreciated the combined support of so many friends. She was grateful to his special friends from the morning coffee group. They were all there and she particularly appreciated the deep expression of loss by Ben Bradshaw, a man she knew Jimmy had cared for and admired as his closest friend. He had been a frequent visitor to their home and, although Ben was quite a few years younger than her husband, they had shared a bond based on strongly held family values and their belief in hard work to get ahead. Ben had held her briefly at the funeral and she had felt his real concern for her and great sorrow at the loss of Jimmy. His offer to help in any way needed was clearly sincere and she thought it demonstrated why Jimmy had thought of him as his best friend.

Meanwhile, the Sheriff's department had been looking at the crash site, doing a careful reconstruction from the available evidence. The tire tracks on the gravel side of the road showed that Jimmy had driven into the fencing on the curve protecting the embankment with great force and had gone through it without braking. There was no evidence of Jimmy's speed other than the car's ability to smash through the fencing before falling down the embankment. There seemed to be no question that he had been traveling at a high rate of speed before the turn. It seemed obvious to the investigators that he had just missed the curve.

The fact that Jimmy's body had been thrown from the car at the crash site was irrefutable evidence that he had failed to use his seat belt before the crash. There was speculation that an animal of some kind had suddenly appeared, and he had attempted to avoid it but nothing supporting that theory was found and that place on the road was not a normal deer crossing due to the cliff preventing access to adjoining woods or food. A close examination of his wrecked car had shown no marks of a collision and gave no additional clues supporting any other conclusion than that Jimmy had met an accidental death caused by speeding at a rate that made it impossible to make the curve.

Alice, assessing the results of the investigation, was totally dissatisfied. She was adamant that Jimmy always wore his seat belt and always slowed down on that section of highway because of the dangerous embankment. They had discussed the minimal guardrail there and had even reported their concerns to the Road Commission long before the crash, but the Commission had failed to reinforce it. Calling the crash an accident made no sense to her and any notion that he had deliberately driven over the edge was laughable. He had been involved in the biggest land development deal in his phenomenally successful profession and was thrilled by the potential profits for him and Alice. The only conclusion that made any sense to her was that he had been murdered.

Her arguments were not taken seriously since murder seemed inconceivable to the police without evidence of some argument or incident that might explain why someone would want him dead. She finally had to accept the routine police report and the coroner's verdict of accidental death, although completely unconvinced. She thought she knew Jimmy better than the police and knew in her heart and mind there had been no accident. It did not add up with the unlocked seat belt, the suggested excess speed, and no evidence of any effort to brake the car.

But why? she asked, over and over. She went through his extensive list of friends and contractors with no answers. She was certain someone had murdered him but could find no whiff of dispute or rancor, only warm friendships, and contractors with no active, unpaid accounts. She thought about her financial condition but was unconcerned since the new subdivision was almost completed with just a few small items left to finish. She had the Bank behind her with Jimmy's friend Dex Henderson in charge. Remembering Dex's guarantee and certain of her strong asset position, Alice planned to meet with him to find out what she needed to do to secure her profits from sales of lots in the new subdivision. Her home was paid for, and she had no worries about eventual sales in the subdivision. Jimmy had left her in a strong financial position, and she was sure Dex would help as he had promised.

Dex was ebullient in his office when she called for an appointment. He was approaching the finish line of his plan and looked forward to it with great anticipation. He would play his part brilliantly and, in a few months, was certain she would be his in every way. He prepared for his performance and, when she walked into his office, it was to a deep embrace and Dex in tears. "What's the matter?" she asked.

He answered with his prepared excuse. "I have terrible news. There has been a shake-up in the Bank's head office and the new board of directors has changed its policy. All its branch presidents have been severely limited in their ability to loan more than a million to anyone without main Bank approval. I was specifically admonished for making your five-million-dollar loan and, although I fought the edict, I have been overruled. Your loan has been called and there is nothing I can do to stop foreclosure if you cannot pay it off right away. I am totally dismayed that I cannot keep your home out of the foreclosure since I guaranteed its protection." Alice was incredulous. "You are telling me that all your promises and your guarantee are no longer viable," she exclaimed.

"I know this is terribly hard for you, but I am going to make sure you are personally taken care of. It is a matter of honor for me and, regardless of the Bank's insane policy change, I will personally make sure you are cared for." She was enraged. "Forget about my home, what can you do to give me time to sell our new subdivision to pay off the line of credit mortgage?" she asked. "Since the loan is in existence, your limitation on giving new loans surely does not apply to me. I will need time to arrange alternative financing to finish the last little things in the subdivision and find a buyer. Some fencing and odds and ends are all I need to finish the finest subdivision in Traverse City, and you know that's true. I can have all of that squared away in ninety days and that is all you must do for me to come out of this nightmare in good financial shape. I will be able to pay off that five million you loaned to buy and build it so the Bank should be satisfied. I need those ninety days and you owe them to me with your guarantee. It is win-win for the Bank and me so there should be no problem with approval of such a brief period of time."

He played the part of an agonized friend to the hilt but told her the Bank had ordered him to call the mortgage and foreclose immediately if she was unable to pay the mortgage off on call. He gave her no caveats, or satisfaction of any kind. He was telling her she had no way out. She was appalled at his refusal to give her time to obtain new financing or sell her subdivision and considered his offer of personal support obscene under the circumstances of what she saw clearly as his betrayal. She had no feelings for him other than her deep anger at his failure to live up to his guarantee and was prepared to belt him if he made further insinuations that she would allow him to care for her. She thought she should belt him anyway but was so upset at his refusal to work with her, she just stormed out of his office and headed home.

She was mad as hell. The Bank commenced foreclosure of all her property within thirty days of Jimmy's death. Dex's unwelcome attentions, including persistent attempts to assuage her grief and anger, added to her growing anger. She realized she was up the proverbial creek without a paddle. She sat alone in their home trying to figure out a solution for the payout of the mortgage and concluded the actions of the Bank were so wrongful, she needed a lawyer. The foreclosure was in progress, and something had to be done. Her efforts to find a buyer had fallen short since the foreclosure had dramatically reduced the potential value and there was no buyer available other than sharks looking to cash in on her dilemma.

Jimmy had always said Ben Bradshaw was the best attorney he had ever known, and she thought of him as her best bet. He had often visited their home and the three of them shared a deep friendship. She had been impressed with his wit and had admired his striking appearance. His presence at Jimmy's funeral and his obvious grief at losing his friend were front and center. She knew she didn't need his help as Jimmy's best friend but as a trial attorney hopefully willing to take on the Bank.

She found his office number in Jimmy's call log while wondering what challenge would surface next and called his office for an appointment. She was angry to the point of thinking about using her old softball bat to smash Dex Henderson's face in. She was still fuming at what she recognized as Dex's crocodile tears.

Ben

Ben Bradshaw had won his reputation for being the best trial lawyer in town in a brief time. He had moved to the city from Detroit with a JD degree from Wayne State University Law School, earned after three years of brutal combat as an Army Ranger. At six feet two and 220 pounds of muscle, he had starred in Wayne State football as a tight end while hitting the books for top billing as a student. He had polished his craft as a trial lawyer with a year's experience in the hurly-burly, incessant action of Detroit's courts. He loved the back and forth of courtroom combat and had the soft voice needed to mask his combativeness. It was this combination with his love of research that had given him victories where the outcome would normally be in doubt. It had not taken his opponents long to understand settling cases with him was smarter than going to trial.

It would have been easy to take advantage of his resume with such a record, but Ben never claimed lofty status and, with true humility, had a few particularly good friends in college who cared for and admired him. He was just one of the guys and never put on the dog for them. From the perspective of the young women he had dated, his blue eyes and reddish-blond hair made the package irresistible. He had not settled on any of them to their individual dismay and, when he thought about it, believed that he would find love later when the right woman came along. This was not to imply he was a poor lover. Quite the contrary, he had enjoyed his times with the gals but had never found the one that rocked his socks as the saying went. Finding that special one was not high on his agenda when he finished law school and moved directly into trial work with a small firm in Detroit.

He loved fishing in Saginaw Bay and had a good buddy, Jerry, who usually fished with him. He had purchased an old, wooden hulled, Marblehead 36-footer for his weekends when he would fish the Michigan shore of Lake Huron. His usual plan was to go up the coast to one of several good marinas on late Friday afternoons and rent a slip for the weekend. Jerry, on a particularly barren result day, suggested trying the east coast of Lake Michigan for the salmon runs. Ben had equipped his boat with downriggers and was intrigued. They decided to take a week boating around the north end of Michigan's Lower Peninsula and ending up at Traverse City as a good place to spend a few days. The trip was uneventful, and they got a transient slip in the city marina at the base of West Bay that gave them walking access to the downtown.

It was Ben's first visit there and he immediately fell in love with the city. He was tremendously pleased by its beautiful, deep, clear bays and the city's forward-looking designation of so much shoreline as parks. The fishing in the bays was reputed as sensational and there were numerous clear water lakes in the area for bass, pike, and walleye fishing, not to mention the salmon runs in Lake Michigan off Michigan's west coast at Leland and south to the Platt River.

He did research on the local courts and was pleased at the fine reputations of the Circuit and District Court Judges.

Thinking that this would be a beautiful place to practice law, he searched out the established law firms and to his pleasant surprise, found one looking for a trial lawyer to add to the firm. They made him an offer to work as their trial lawyer if he was ready to move sooner rather than later. It was a no-brainer for Ben. He made the decision to move almost immediately, his memories of his frustration in Detroit Court trials being a major influence. His interview was outstanding and the firm hired him as a welcome addition.

The firm had him in the local courts immediately and he found it an exciting change to try cases before Judges with topflight legal scholarship after his frustration at practicing before Judges in Detroit where politics ran the courts and incompetence was expected from the Judges and exhibited all too often by the bar. After two successful and happy years with the Traverse City firm, he opened his own office with the firm's blessing and best wishes. They were less pleased when he took their best, young secretary, Sherry, with him. She was so sharp he turned over his office to her and let her handle all the client meetings, court appearances and the office checkbook. He hoped his reputation, earned with wins in several high-profile cases, would provide enough clients to pay the bills.

He found himself more than a little jealous of guys like Jimmy who found the love of their life. His and Alice's idyllic and loving marriage inspired him. He had not found his dream girl yet but, when he occasionally thought about it, remained hopeful. His folks did not bug him about it, but he knew they hoped he would find someone to marry sooner than later. After all, they thought, he was only a couple of years before thirty. Moving from Detroit had cut down the pool of available women his age quite sharply and he had not really made much of a dent in his new town's social life. His primary source of information about the town and possible dates was the coffee group he managed to attend most weekday mornings at the Park Place Hotel. His friends covered all the local news and social events regularly and in detail. He had come to know a few of the local women his age and had enjoyed several dates, but not to the point of wanting to go further romantically.

It pleased him that his friends were willing to talk politics although Ben was only one of three Democrats at the table in Republican Traverse City and had a lot of defending to do for the Democratic minority. They tended to gang up on him because they knew he liked the discussions. He enjoyed the badinage and held his own most of the time. Having opened his own office, he spent long hours making his occasional clients happy and, most evenings, was in his office working. He knew he had developed a good reputation at trial but also knew his preparation was the key to continued success. His usual, intense case research didn't give him much time for dating.

Ben had become Jimmy's best friend and was particularly happy about his luck in finding Alice. He enjoyed his frequent times with them. They were as liberal in their politics as Ben and Jimmy was happier than Ben had ever seen him. Ben thought the coffee group foolish when they remained a little jealous of Jimmy's having found his dream girl and thought Alice could have done much better. Ben knew that was baloney. He admired his friend and let the group know they were off base. Not that Jimmy was not still trim and physically active at 35, but he had not been suspected of having such a different side as a bon vivant or sensualist. There were joking remarks suggesting he would have difficulty living up to Alice's youthful enthusiasm although the consensus was complimentary. His friends just envied him his luck and wished him well. Jimmy was a good guy and very well liked throughout the community.

Ben had been in his own office for a brief time and was only twenty-six when he had been invited to Jimmy Jones' wedding, and, tragically, within less than two years, his funeral. Having been advised of his appointment with Alice the next morning, his mind jumped back to her wedding. He remembered his reaction to her blazing red hair and her height. Ben stood at six feet two himself and had never dated a woman as tall as Alice who was at least five feet nine without heels. When he had been introduced at the reception, he had found himself mesmerized by her green eyes, sparkling, he thought, like the famous emerald he had seen in photos from a major European museum. He had believed her eyes matched the beauty of that gem and, over the next almost two years as Jimmy's best friend, had found his original assessment accurate. She had become a wonderful friend and the three of them had enjoyed their many evenings together.

With her request for an appointment, he assumed it was regarding the Bank's foreclosure. He had been surprised to hear how soon after Jimmy's death the Bank had foreclosed and had thought it was shameful at best. He found himself looking forward to seeing her again, even as a grieving widow. He wondered if there was anything that could be done to help her. He thought Dex was sharp in Bank matters and had little doubt all the i's had been dotted and the t's crossed in the foreclosure proceedings. Challenging foreclosures was generally a losing proposition since they were technical and statutorily driven.

The New Alice

Sherry had told Alice to come into Ben's office at 8 AM and she walked into his office precisely at eight. Ben's heart almost stopped from the impact of her youthful beauty and obvious anger. This was a new Alice. She was mad, and those green eyes pierced him like lasers. "Do you have any idea why I am here?" she said. "I know a little from public discussion if it's about the Bank's foreclosure," he answered. She sagged and collapsed into a chair in front of him. Her story began and it was in a rush of words so fast they were difficult to follow.

She was enraged at Dex Henderson who, she said, "had promised she would keep her home and not be harmed by the Bank on their mortgage. He had given his personal guarantee to back up his promises. We would never have signed the mortgage without Dex's specific guarantee. Now he has betrayed me and is taking everything I own."

Ben interrupted by saying "that the odds on beating the foreclosures are astronomical against you. Tell me again what Dex guaranteed." She told the story more clearly, again featuring her astonishment at Dex's perfidy.

"It all seems to go back to Jimmy's death," he said. "I know very little about the circumstances of that. Were there any questions raised about it?" She looked up and he was amazed at the change he saw. She had been angry, but his question lit a spark in her eyes that had not been there when she walked into his office. She sat up straighter and made consistent eye contact as she answered. "I am certain it was impossible for the crash to have been an accident as ruled by the coroner. Jimmy never drove over the speed limit and never without his seat belt fastened. He was obsessive about it. He always took special care on that section of highway, and we had complained about it to the Road Commission. I checked with the dealer and Jimmy's new car had been serviced a week or so before and was in perfect condition according to the mechanics. I am certain it didn't happen the way it has been officially described but the police have written it off as an accident caused by Jimmy speeding. I have no idea who would have killed him since I believe everyone liked him and there are no disputes or money problems that might have led to murder. Without any discernible motive, there is nowhere to go except that I know, without a shadow of a doubt, it was no accident. He was murdered."

Ben was surprised and impressed with her conclusions and wondered aloud who profited from the crash. The only clear financial winner was the Third Michigan Bank and Trust, and Ben thought it was impossible to imagine a murder committed by a financial institution with so many people involved in the Bank's hierarchy. It would be impossible to keep such an explosive secret.

An errant thought popped up and he wondered whether the Bank's ownership of the property sold to Jimmy could be attacked. If there had been violations in the Bank's original foreclosure, it would invalidate the Bank's title and he could set aside the sale to Jimmy and Alice. His curiosity had been aroused at the news of that foreclosure when the story in the Record Eagle had indicated the original owner had been quite old. He thought it was a possible line of attack if the Bank had not acted appropriately with a senior citizen although he thought it improbable at best. With the Bank's solid basis for foreclosure of Alice's property, it didn't look promising.

Since Dex was the lead for the Bank, and she had expressed her anger at what she saw as betrayal, Ben asked about him and whether he had been in contact with her after the foreclosure had begun. The answer was compelling and indicated more to him than she might be happy to hear. She told him, "Dex has tried to be supportive to the point of coming to my home unexpectedly and uninvited on several evenings." Ben followed up, asking, "Has he been personally attentive in the sense of coming on to you?" She was surprised at his question and took some time before answering. Her answer was reflective after her pause. "I never thought of Dex in that context. The man is forty years old with a pot belly and there is nothing attractive about him. His money is all he has going for him and might get him women looking for that style of life. I admit I have become concerned about his attentions. He always seems to be near me, suggesting he wants me to lean on him during this period of grief. Even suggesting I will live with him in his spacious home after losing my home. I am angry at his attention. It is because of his promises that I am in this mess today and nothing could be clearer than the fact he has not lived up to them. I want no part of him. He betrayed us. I have not told him how I feel in specific language and admit I wanted to hit him in his lying mouth when he clearly thought I would accept his personal care to the point of having me live in his home when my home was eventually taken in the foreclosure. Since it was certain I was going to lose my home, it was an offer made with an intended result and that bothered me. He is a first-class asshole by any definition."

Ben enjoyed her assessment of Dex and could see that the idea of Dex having intentions for her was an idea that had never really occurred to her. Her answers had him convinced Dex was on the make but that did not seem relevant to the foreclosures, and he didn't share his conclusion with her. Ben had started the conversation on a regular fact-finding approach, but it had become so personal he was astonished. She was the most charming woman he had ever encountered, and he had learned long ago, was highly intelligent as well. She was talking increasingly freely and the initial concerns she had were gone between them. Ben took a moment to express his personal grief at her loss of Jimmy and how much he had admired him as his friend. "I know how much you miss him and his counsel in your financial chaos from this attack by the Bank."

She answered honestly and in great depth. "Jimmy was so dynamic and thoughtful I agreed when he proposed, thinking our marriage would be perfect. Our age difference didn't seem important to me, but he seemed always aware of it and was a passionate husband. After a very short time we became full partners in the land development business. I think initially, he saw me as a prize, but he had fallen as hard for me as I for him. We shared almost two years of love and mutual respect. I miss him every moment and he would be pleased that I am meeting with you. He said you were the best attorney in town and, just like Jimmy, I have enjoyed our friendship."

Ben asked, "Do you want me to represent you and attempt a defense to the Bank's foreclosure?" The answer was a resounding "yes." He shared his notion that the first foreclosure by the Bank involved an aged woman, and he intended investigating the circumstances of that action. He told her, "If the Bank did not get a clean title, they couldn't sell her land to you. It sems to me the prior owner was incredibly old and there is a possibility her cognitive abilities were compromised to the extent the Bank should have known and acted differently. Due to her age, the Bank should have been worried about the size of her transaction if for no other reason. It required a strong investigation by the Bank, and we don't know if that was done. On the other hand, my impression is that you and Jimmy signed your mortgage and there doesn't seem a basis for preventing that foreclosure except by challenging the original foreclosure of the land the Bank sold you and Jimmy.

"It will be an explosive avenue to attack the Bank's sale to you and the current foreclosures on that basis, but it will give us a clean shot at any negligence of the Bank in its treatment of the prior owner. It is only common sense that a Bank would have routinely made sure she did not have cognitive difficulty.

Whether the Bank used common sense will be the basis for our strong investigation. If we can prove the Bank failed to provide good title to you, it will defeat the foreclosure of your property and take care of the substantial losses you face. If the Bank was negligent, it will give you a terrific lawsuit with a good chance of a major verdict.

Bring me all the paperwork you have from the Bank on the foreclosure of your land, and I will go through it to see if there is anything wrong with their procedure. I doubt there will be because the Bank's lawyer will have filed so many of them. However, their claims will give me a starting point in any event.

We need that deep, complete investigation of the circumstances of the foreclosure of the original owner of the land the Bank sold Jimmy and you. If we can find a hint of mistake, negligence, or deliberate action on the part of the Bank regarding her cognitive ability, we will have a chance for an Injunction stopping your foreclosure until the matter is covered in the final trial.

I know an investigator who has the tenacity and ability to look into this and, hopefully, he will be available for the job. His name is Joe Binds, and his background is as a Sergeant with the State Police. He retired with a bullet wound that gave him too great a disability to continue as an active officer and has been working as a PI since. I have worked with him and trust his judgment and abilities. I will ask him to begin our look at that first foreclosure. If it smells, we will track down the source of the odor. I realize you are currently low on funds and don't want you to be concerned about any indebtedness to me. Jimmy was my best friend and I have spent so many lovely evenings with you both, I count you as my special friend as well. I owe it to Jimmy and you to fight this foreclosure and will take care of all expenses up front until the case is completed. If there are expenses due then, we will work that out as friends, and you have my guarantee you will not be harmed. I am not Dex. My guarantee is real."

She had listened intently and the initial sag in her shoulders had disappeared. "I will bring in everything I have on the foreclosure. I know your guarantee is real and appreciate your concern for me. I will do whatever you need from me and am suddenly more confident we will have a shot at the Bank. Thank you, Ben." The following day she signed the fee agreement Sherry had prepared and thought her signature was the first step on the way to showing Dex how she felt about his brutal handling of her. She had found enormous relief from her meeting with

Ben. She saw him accurately as the special friend her husband Jimmy had made and admired. She thought if anyone could stop the Bank, it would be Ben.

Ben began by sorting out her statement about Jimmy's death. Her belief the circumstances of the crash were suspicious and pointed inexorably to murder, was clearly rational. He realized that, if she was right and he thought she was, she might be targeted. There was no clear motive for murder but, assuming her husband was killed, the wife might be next on some list. Why only Jimmy? He realized there was no guarantee she was not targeted as well for a later time.

He had his carry permit from the ugly days in Detroit's courts, with its dubious at best Defendants, and decided to purchase a pair of compact Glock 19s that could be carried without showing their presence. His old service revolver was too heavy and visible for his purpose. He went into Benzie County to a gun shop and went through the required legal procedures to buy two small and light editions of the famous automatics, and 9-mm luger rounds that fit them. While there he looked over the considerable line of protection equipment and was pleased to find the latest model of Kevlar vests guaranteed to stop anything but an armor piercing military round. It was standard police issue, light in weight and slim enough to wear without anyone knowing it was there. He bought two and, a week later, had his Glocks. With the smaller Glock in his hand, he had a flashback to the time when he had managed to shoot himself out of a jam. It had been one of several gunfights he had survived. He remembered so many of his war-time experiences and could feel that intensity coming back.

He felt better with the gun in hand although there was no way to see an attack coming. They had no idea who was involved or why. He thought that if they ever learned the motive, they would be surprised. It had to be off the wall in some way but that didn't reduce the current danger. The attack had not been on Alice, and he took some comfort from that for the moment.

It had been only a few days since their last meeting when he called Alice and asked her to come to the office. She was there within a half-hour, and he told her for the first time, his concerns that she might be in danger. "Why?" she asked. He told her, "You have convinced me that Jimmy was murdered, and my first question is, why Jimmy alone? You were both owners of a subdivision having a value of millions of dollars and it is possible Jimmy's death came from that development in some way. If so, you may be next on someone's list. I don't think I share the risk but, in our state of bewilderment, it makes sense for us both to defend ourselves. I have bought Kevlar vests for us both and small, light Glock automatics that we can carry without anyone knowing we have them. I will take you to a shooting range to practice and teach you all about your gun. I have used guns to survive, and you will be ready to defend yourself after a few hours of practice. The vests are designed to be worn under regular clothes and, again, no one will know we have them."

She agreed immediately and he arranged to pick her up for range practice the next morning. She said, "I will be wearing my vest from this moment forward. I can't find the right words or enough of them to thank you." He found a range fifty miles away where he was sure they would not be identified. She practiced with her Glock, and he was astonished at her quick mastering of the gun. She was no expert but could place her bullet in the body of the target over and over at twenty feet. It was a fun morning, and they found a little roadside restaurant for lunch.

"You know," she said, "I really don't know much about you even though the three of us spent a lot of time together." She began by asking about his family. He talked for a long time about his parents, his brothers and his growing up in upstate New York. He was proud of his loving family, and it was plain, as he described them, how much he cared. She wanted to know all about his growing up and asked several questions that brought out stories of things he had enjoyed and his sports activities in high school. He told her about the little village in western New York he had grown up in and how pretty it was with a creek running through, servicing woolen mills and paper mills. How it had inspired his love of fishing as well as the skinny dipping he and his friends had enjoyed in the clay bends of nine-mile creek.

She wanted to know about his army service. He never had talked in any depth about his combat experience but found himself telling her more than he had ever disclosed to anyone else, including his brothers. His stories were difficult to tell, and she listened with compassion to his accounts of friends lost. He found himself opening up in a way he never had with anyone before about his Ranger service and various survival stories. She continued to press him for his thoughts on issue after issue. He told her about his strong hatred of racism and how his friends in combat never gave a rat's ass what a man's color was who fought beside them and had their back. He was appalled at homelessness and hoped to do something about it. He had already worked with several agencies on solutions in Traverse City. "Sleeping under the bridge over the Boardman River downtown behind the Bank building," he said, "is tough but not the worst situation the homeless face in our town."

She then answered his questions about her background, showing her love for her sister and parents. He was not

surprised to hear that she had excelled in school and graduated summa cum laude from Central Michigan University.
She had been a four-year player on its topflight softball
team, and it was obvious from her shared memories, had
finished as one of its stars although she made light of her
accomplishments. He had observed her athletic carriage
and was impressed at her abilities. He told her about playing
football at Wayne State and three sports in high school. She
was extremely impressed with his Juris Doctor from Wayne
State Law School, and, in a final linking of their histories,
both enjoyed discussing politics as strong, liberal Democrats.

He suddenly grinned and asked, "how do you feel
about fishing." She laughed and answered, "I wondered
when you were going to ask since Jimmy told me you had
a boat in the marina and loved to fish. He told me in a joking way because he knew I loved to fish, and he could get
a rise out of me. Jimmy didn't care for fishing at all and,
although I never held it against him, he kidded me a bit.
The truth is I have been fishing since I was a toddler with
my dad. We lived on a small lake in southern Michigan
that has good sized bass, bluegills, and crappies with a few
big pike thrown in, and I loved it. My sister Lena is a good
fisherman also. She brought in a pike that weighed almost
fifteen pounds last year and then put it back to grow some
more. When Jimmy kidded me, I told him he had to set up
a fishing trip with you on your boat but we got so involved
in the new subdivision, we never followed through."

Ben suddenly realized he was having the best day since
coming to Traverse City and credited his enjoyable holiday
from his usual working day to his delightful companion.

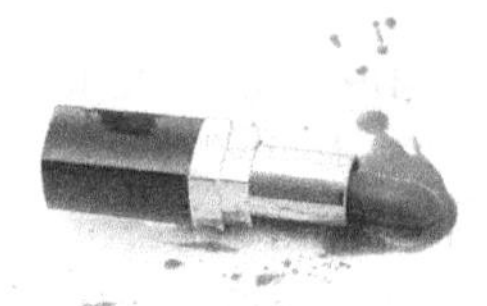

Joe Binds

He reached Joe on his first attempt and was pleased Joe indicated he was available right away. Ben scheduled a meeting with him the next day and Ben, Alice and Joe met for breakfast and went over what Ben wanted regarding the original foreclosure of Jane Bishop. "I want anything indicating loss of cognitive ability and I want to know every individual who saw her or met with her for the six months before she signed that mortgage the Bank foreclosed on. If you can, get statements from anyone who met with her during those six months. She had a substantial estate according to the grapevine and I want to know why she couldn't pay off her mortgage. If Dex Henderson's name surfaces at any point, follow that lead. I don't know what his part has been in all of this, but I have a strong hunch he is the key. If possible, try to find evidence establishing the number of his meetings with her, if any. We need anything that indicates knowledge on the part of the Bank regarding her cognitive condition. If she had failed or was failing, we need when and testimony regarding the depth of the loss. With witnesses who can establish that we have a shot at winning."

Ben gave Joe a retainer to start and guaranteed Joe's fees in the investigation although Joe made it clear his experience with Ben was sufficient to ensure payment. His final words emphasized his feelings. "Glad to be working with you again, Ben, as always it feels good, and Alice, it's great to meet you. You have the best trial attorney in the state."

Alice had been doing a lot of thinking about Dex Henderson and had concluded that his actions were strange at best. When Ben added his name to Joe's search, she found herself wondering what in hell Dex had been thinking in his so-called "caring moments." It was more than strange, and she shared that assessment with Ben who had already concluded Dex Henderson was involved in some way. They waited now for Joe's investigation in hopes it would give them a leg up on a defense and a basis for requesting an Injunction stopping the foreclosure of Alice's land. If it existed, it would be a whole new ballgame and Ben could see a potential lawsuit for damages to Alice, including the loss of her property and loss of profits on the subdivision she and Jimmy had been close to finishing. He knew several appraisers who would give expert testimony if needed. It wouldn't take much evidence of the Bank's negligence to support a massive judgment for Alice against the Bank.

Joe Reports

Joe called almost two weeks later and said he needed to meet immediately. Ben called Alice and they met Joe in Ben's office within an hour of Joe's call. He was obviously excited when he walked in, and it didn't take long to realize why when he started.

"I obtained statements from two nurses who had daily contact with Jane Bishop, and both signed a statement under oath that Jane was completely gone cognitively for a year before she signed the mortgage. They said that she didn't recognize her children or the nurses from day to day, that she was in a near vegetative state for the last six months and there had been no lucid moments for more than a minute or two they had observed in the better part of the year before her death. Each of them said they had observed visits by Dex Henderson during that year and particularly during the last six months prior to her death but had assumed he was just there to review documents in her files. They both agreed there was no possibility for Jane to have made a lucid decision relating to financial matters or her property during the six months prior to her death and that there was no apparent physical reason for her death since her vitals were strong, and she was under no stress.

Her doctor had stopped visiting her at the beginning of the year before her death and both nurses said he had determined there was no need for regular doctor visits since she was physically healthy, and they were applying the salves for any irritation on her skin. They were recommending to the family that Jane should be moved into a final rest home. Her children had made the arrangements, and the move would have been made just a few days after her untimely death. They both told me they were stunned at her sudden death since there was no indication of any condition that would cause a death so soon, and certainly not from dementia."

Ben and Alice were ecstatic at Joe's story. It established a scenario where Henderson, as a representative of the Bank, must have known about Jane's loss of cognitive ability to support the foreclosed mortgage. The Bank had obtained signatures from a demented individual, incapable of making a lucid decision or signing any document, which was the basis for the original foreclosure of her land. Although the financial gains to the Bank were evident, it was difficult at best to see a motive for such a clear scam of Jane Bishop. The unusual circumstances of her death were troubling but there seemed no connection except in a coincidental comparison with Jimmy's death, also ruled as accidental or without clear explanation. The deaths were related only when put in a timeline without an apparent connection on its face, but Ben was unconvinced there was no real connection. Two deaths directly related to a Bank foreclosure were more than troubling regardless of whether he and Alice could imagine a motive.

It was obvious to all of them that Joe's report called for further investigation of the basic scam against Jane Bishop and a series of depositions of the Bank's employees including Dex Henderson. It was time to file a Complaint against the Bank with a request for a temporary injunction that would stop Alice's foreclosure pending the final trial. Ben thought he had sufficient testimony to convince a Judge relief was needed until all the facts were settled with a trial verdict. Temporary Injunctions were a normal instrument a circuit Judge would consider issuing to protect the status quo before a final verdict by a jury. Ben thought he could make a strong enough argument with Joe's information to convince the Judge to issue the injunction.

Obtaining copies of the checks drawn on Jane's account was now at the top of the agenda and Ben worked on his demand for those documents as part of his preparation of the initial filing. He intended to demand a jury trial to make sure the selection process for the Judge did not affect the final verdict.

Ben had been thinking about a potential Complaint for some time while waiting and hoping for Joe's report. He had only hope for a basis until Joe's revelations. He had what he needed now to file the request for preliminary relief halting the foreclosure of Alice's property pending disposition of the new claim that the Bank had proceeded on a scam mortgage, whether known or unknown. He would feature the scamming of Jane Bishop and demand copies of Jane's checks. For the first time, Ben and Alice had a hook for litigation but it was incomplete without Jane's children's testimony. It seemed certain they would be in full support and anxious to help and Ben thought they should be contacted and brought up to speed on the Bank's actions.

Lawsuit

Ben contacted **John Bishop** who immediately indicated he, his brother and sister would want to join any litigation on Jane's foreclosure. Ben suggested they hire their own attorney since there might be differences in approach and an additional attorney would be helpful. He received a call within three hours from Harold Brown, a local attorney Ben liked and respected. They agreed to meet the next day and went over the possibilities together for an hour or two. Alice was overjoyed at the additional Plaintiffs and their attorney coming on board. She made it plain she had total faith in Ben but they both agreed this was progress and were pleased at Harold's entry into the Complaint process and goals of the suit.

The meeting with Harold and the Bishop heirs was very cordial from the first moments of introduction. Although John Bishop had made a strong effort to get police action on what he called a scam on his mother, they had no additional information beyond the mortgage amount and the foreclosure papers. They had visited Jane in the year before her death and confirmed that she had been in the throes of dementia to the point of not recognizing them and unable to speak words or sentences at all for a year before her death. They said it was pitiful and her nurses had recommended placing her in a home since she was completely unable to care for herself, could not dress and could not perform her bouts on the toilet. The mortgage had been a complete surprise, not just because of its huge amount but because they could not imagine her having the ability to sign it after they had seen her dementia firsthand.

Ben shared Joe's report with them and his intent to file against the Bank on Jane's foreclosure as his attack on the Bank's sale to Alice and Jimmy. They quickly understood that success in setting aside the mortgage and foreclosure of their mother's property would potentially be a strong financial result for them although they seemed more interested in fighting for their mother's reputation. They were enthusiastic supporters of attacking the Bank and Harold offered immediate help in any way Ben needed. Ben asked him to prepare affidavits as exhibits for each of the Bishops for attachment to the initial Complaint they were preparing to file. Harold agreed and said the affidavits would be ready the next day. Ben suggested that Harold have the Bishop children join Alice's suit as co-Plaintiffs and that he and Harold meet in three days to work on their joint complaint. He told Harold he would have his proposed complaint ready for their meeting by then.

When they met, Ben found Harold was exceptionally capable and they worked together easily. They finished the Complaint and turned it over for typing to Sherry. Harold's secretary had already finished the affidavits and all three Bishops had signed theirs. Ben wanted to file their joint action in three days. When it was ready for filing, Ben and Harold signed it for their respective clients and Ben filed it along with their Petition for Preliminary Injunctive Relief stopping the foreclosure of Alice's property pending proofs on the original foreclosure by the Bank on Jane's property.

The affidavits of all three Bishop children were a strong basis for injunctive relief.

It had been ten days since receiving Joe's report. Ben made a Discovery request amounting to a demand, for copies of Jane's checks for the year before her death as a part of the filing. He and Harold agreed on the witnesses needed for their motion and filed an additional motion for depositions of the Bank's employees including the President and board of directors of the Third Michigan Bank and Trust and its Traverse City branch, as well as Dex Henderson. They knew there would be a prompt response, given the amount of money involved.

There would have been considerable concern for their safety if they could have seen the murderous rage Dex Henderson was in. He had just learned Alice was being seen often with Ben Bradshaw and he blew a gasket thinking how that slimy attorney had moved in on her. He realized he had a new problem outside his original plan, and his anger was so intense he was having difficulty making sense of what he should do about it. As time passed, he calmed down a bit and began resurrecting his sly ideas about finally bringing her to her senses. It was plain to him that Ben had caught her in a moment of grief and had promised to care for her, just as he had, expecting her to come to him quite soon. He was mad that Ben was making the same move on Alice he had planned but was sure it was a momentary thing for her and his position as the real person who cared for her the most would eventually cancel this wayward event. Competition with a dull young attorney was beneath him and unnecessary with his eventual winning of Alice so much a sure thing.

He realized this complication could add more time to his plans for Alice and concluded that Ben would have to be disposed of, just as Jimmy had been, but in a different manner. He knew Ben had Ranger experience but had gained great confidence in his hired killer and was sure he could do the job despite Ben's experience in combat. He would make sure his hired killer knew all of that so the hit would go as planned.

Response

Dex **went to his office** on Monday and was met by his chief of staff with Ben's Complaint. It included a demand for copies of all checks drawn on Jane Bishop's account for the year preceding her death and Ben's request for Preliminary Injunctive relief. Dex was inflamed at Ben's presumption. He hid his anger easily and took the Complaint into his office to review it.

The demand for copies of the checks was troublesome but he knew his forgeries were a perfect match. Dex, after having been given his position as President of the local branch by his father, had no interest in attending seminars on appropriate Banking procedures to discover forgeries. He had practiced forging Jane's signature and assumed, with his incredible IQ, he knew everything important regarding Banking, including forgeries.

He was confident his signatures on Jane's documents were perfect and the money he had amassed could not be traced to him. It was clear to him that everyone's conclusion would be that the scammer had been clever and successful. He laughed as he thought how unable the police would be to put his puzzle together. Dealing with so many dull people was worth a laugh, and he made sure his office was closed and soundproof before he had the belly laugh this whole exercise deserved. The joint complaint of the Bishops and Alice would be demolished in the courtroom for a complete lack of evidence. He looked forward to his joust with Ben Bradshaw and the final humiliation Bradshaw would suffer at his hands. The notion that anyone, much less a young and dull attorney, could fence successfully with him was ridiculous to him considering the tremendous gap he perceived in their intelligence. "Ben has no idea what he faces with me," he said to the empty office.

The Bank's attorney had been called immediately when the Bank was served and came into Dex's office a short time after Dex had finished his laughter. George Faltner had been the Bank's attorney for years and had filed both foreclosures that were the basis for the lawsuit. He had easily handled routine litigation for the Bank, and his first question to Dex cut to the heart of Ben's Complaint.

"What was the cognitive condition of Jane Bishop when she signed that mortgage we foreclosed? I know you said she was lucid when she took out her mortgage to build those houses for her kids, but Bradshaw is claiming she had been cognitively dysfunctional for more than a year before that deal and we are looking at a potential 'he said, she said' scenario where the Bank could look very bad in court."

It was at that precise moment when Dex's phone rang and he was faced with a direct inquiry from his father, Dexter Henderson, President of the Bank with offices in Lansing, Michigan. He opened his call with, "I have been informed that a lawsuit has been filed against the Bank alleging negligence in the treatment of a senior citizen by your branch office. The case appears to involve a mortgage we foreclosed. Is this a case we should be concerned about, or can it be settled for a few thousand dollars? We don't need litigation and avoid it when possible since it screws up our PR badly."

Dex had flipped his phone to speaker and answered them both. "There is no need for concern," he said. "I met with Jane Bishop on several occasions during the period the lawsuit claims she had lost her cognitive abilities and, although she was usually tired and a little weak, there was no question in my mind that she was planning a great surprise for her kids and the mortgage funds were intended to make that happen. I don't think anyone plans such a project while incapacitated. I doubt there is anyone else with a history with her capable of supporting a dispute over her plans. If her kids testify it will obviously be greed talking and I doubt the court will be much impressed.

She showed me preliminary drawings from the company in Ohio and said that the contractor had impressed her with his professionalism. She told me she had met with him several times and had been shown pictures of beautiful homes he had built. She also told me she had talked with a solid purchaser of the part of her land not required for the new homes and would have the funds to pay off the mortgage in plenty of time. She had decided this wonderful gift for her kids was worth more to her than her strong love for her home and land. I really liked Jane and it was obvious she was intending to make sure her estate benefited her children. She knew, at 93, she had a looming deadline to finish her plans and openly acknowledged it."

"That's all well and good," his father said. "These lawsuits are usually intended to force a settlement and involve little more than a good payday for the attorney. You should consider settling it." Dex responded angrily, "that a settlement was not wise where the litigation was based on greed." His father just said, "Handle it the best way you determine. It's your baby. We won't worry about it so long as you are confident you have it contained."

He hung up and George chimed in, "The problem is that Ben Bradshaw is the best trial attorney in town and court is where he makes his living. You will need to be prepared for a cross examination on these points in your deposition and at trial. He will be scheduling the depositions soon and we need to be ready. I like Ben. He is a straight shooter and there is always the possibility of a settlement that works for us as well as his client. He's not a hot dog trying to make a name for himself through trials in all his cases."

Dex blew that out of the water. "I will not consider settlement. Let him try to break me down. I was there with her, and this case will never fly. I know the law regarding agreements with cognitively challenged people and she was not challenged. I can handle this young pup Bradshaw easily. He has been in town for only a couple of years, and I have been here for seven years. The jury will believe me when I present the true facts."

George was perplexed and professionally challenged by Dex's position but not in a strong position to argue. After all, Dex was speaking for the Bank, and he had just heard the Bank's President turn management of the lawsuit over to Dex. It struck him that Dex had a hell of an ego problem bordering on arrogance that would not go over well with a jury. He fervently hoped for a settlement offer that would change Dex's mind and prevent a courtroom confrontation between him and Ben. Regardless of Dex's conceit, George knew Ben would be a tough foe and it was going to be a rough day in court for the Bank if Dex continued to be so dense about the potential harm from public airing of the Bank's actions.

With Dex committed to defending the complaint for Injunctive relief that would stop the current foreclosure of Alice's property, George had no choice but to deny all allegations of the Complaint and wait for a scheduled hearing on the request for Preliminary relief. He filed the Bank's Answer within the required fifteen days. The Defendant Bank was not required to turn over the checks for another month or so.

The initial hearing would be scheduled by the court and, since they represented the Plaintiffs, Ben and Harold would present their witnesses before the Bank could present its testimony in opposition.

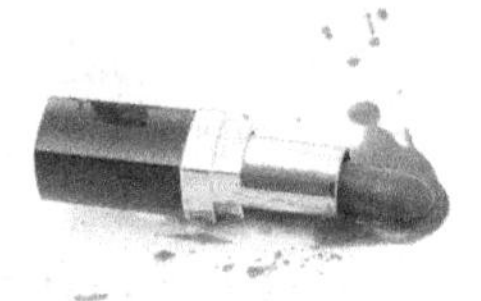

Preliminary Motion

Ben and Harold discussed their approach and agreed Ben would cross exam the Bank's witnesses and argue the case while Harold would present the Bishops' testimony first. He would be lead counsel regarding their testimony and whatever cross examination the Bank attempted. Ben thought Harold one of the best trial attorneys in town and had no reservations as to his ability to present the Bishops as solid citizens who were more interested in how badly they believed their mother had been treated than the money. Harold would go over their testimony, and it should be effective, since they had visited their mother regularly, to support a finding of their love for her rather than any anticipated inheritance. As to money, their joint Complaint requested damages including punitive damages from the Bank for its grossly negligent and improper foreclosure of Jane's land and subsequent sale and fraudulent foreclosure of Alice.

Ben planned his cross examination of the Bank's witnesses or witness on whatever claim the Bank made regarding contact with Jane immediately prior to the massive mortgage and during the year before her death. If he could establish the appearance of negligence on the part of the Bank in its foreclosure of Jane Bishop's land, he felt sure they could obtain the preliminary relief stopping Alice's foreclosure.

He would move from that line of inquiry to questioning the Bank's witnesses regarding Jane's Bank account. He wanted to know the number of checks drawn during the year before her death and where the mortgage money had gone. He was sure there would be a series of objections from the Bank, but the information was at the core of the Complaint. He and Harold looked forward to the Bank employees' answers as potentially the lynchpin of their case. He was confident Judge Hacket, the Circuit Court Judge assigned to their suit, would allow extensive cross examination.

Both Ben and Harold had considerable experience in Judge Hacket's court and had the same belief that the Judge was not only fair but extremely capable. He had been elected for two terms so far and had demonstrated a strong sense of compassion for senior litigants before him where necessary. They were thrilled that he was their assigned Judge as they believed he had the ability to see through flim-flam and that his essential fairness would make him enraged at any action taking advantage of an advanced age senior. Hacket's well-known approach would be disciplined with strict control of counsel's usual attempts to take over the trial. Ben and Harold both liked that approach.

Ben was planning his approach after the Bank's testimony was finished and he had seen the Bank's defense. He knew the Bank would have to claim Jane had cognitive ability sufficient to support her mortgage and he looked forward to his cross examination of the Bank's witness or witnesses and learning for the first-time what actions the Bank believed justified the huge mortgage and what investigation it had made of her condition.

He concluded that, after the Bank witnesses were finished, he would call the nurses as rebuttal witnesses. He would put each of the two nurses on the stand to blast the Bank with their evidence of Jane's total loss of cognitive ability for at least a year before her death. The nurses' testimony that she was incapable of signing her name, much less understanding her finances, would be dynamite against the Bank's position. The nurses, Eva Gantry and Sharon Cowles, had both said that they had observed Jane's effort to write with a pen early in the year and the result both had seen was a series of meaningless scribbles including apparent attempts to sign the page. The attempted signatures had been incomplete and misspelled, written in much larger, backward letters totally different from the signatures they had witnessed more than a year before. They would testify that Jane had never picked up the pen again and had evidenced no interest in the pages she scribbled on in the early part of the year before her death. The Bank's claim would be blown out of the water if there were checks drawn over her purported signature during her total loss of cognitive ability. If there were documents or checks signed by her in that year, it would be obvious the signatures were forgeries and that a scam had been in progress. Harold would be looking to overturn Jane's foreclosure due to the Bank's clear failure to protect her while Ben would be using that testimony to stop Alice's foreclosure.

They had filed the affidavits of John Bishop, David Bishop, and Sylvia Bishop Turner in support of the motion for Preliminary Relief, holding the names and the testimony of the two visiting nurses back. Their testimony would be the clincher since Ben and Harold expected the Bank would cross examine Jane's kids on their knowledge of the property value and argue their testimony was a blatant, self-serving attempt to get Jane's property back for the family. The property had a minimum value of close to three million and they had no doubt the Bank would be arguing greed had raised its ugly head.

They knew the Bank would have to rebut the Bishops' testimony and the nurses would be powerful witnesses to give rebuttal testimony as non-partisan observers who had daily opportunities to observe her condition over the year prior to her death. Their period of observation included every date on which Jane might have supposedly written a check on her account during that year, including what-ever she had done with the mortgage money. It was an assumption since they had not yet seen her checks during that period. Ben knew the details of her mortgage because they had been part of the Bank's sale to Jimmy but had not received copies of her checks since discovery in the main case had not started yet. He was flying blind on how her mortgage had come to be.

The thrust of his argument was going to be gross neg-ligence on the part of the Bank in allowing a 93-year-old woman, living alone, to execute a mortgage for such a large amount without adequately checking on her mental condition. He had no idea what kind of investigation and evaluation the Bank had made and looked forward to the Bank's testimony. It would be a turning point in his favor if the Bank had not performed a review in some depth prior to lending her nine hundred thousand dollars. He was more and more confident that Jane's foreclosure smelled bad, and concluded Alice had a stronger chance of stop-ping her foreclosure than he had thought when he took her case. Joe's report had been the powerful bomb destroy-ing the Bank's position, if it was based on proving Jane was able to sign the mortgage the Bank had foreclosed.

They had filed the demand for a jury trial and Ben had found his enthusiasm growing for Alice's position and the potential for a jury inflamed at Jane's treatment. He knew it would carry over for Alice and the potential damages were much larger than his original estimate when he had assumed the Bank would have a strong legal position on both foreclosures.

Judge Hacket set the hearing date for the Plaintiffs' Motion for a Preliminary Injunction in three weeks on the first half-day available. It was a busy three weeks as Ben, Harold and Alice met daily for several hours swapping ideas and planning the final trial. Ben and Alice found it convenient to have lunch and, usually, dinner together. Their friendship was growing stronger by the day, and she had found he was remarkably capable of clearing her head from her grief at her loss of Jimmy. He was always so positive it rubbed off and she was rapidly becoming happier than she had thought possible in such a relatively short time. He had originally intended to suggest she go south to stay with her parents to help ensure her safety, but their continued daily working together had made it seem foolish. He thought he could protect her and didn't fully realize how much his decision was dictated by his enjoyment of her presence. Just as Jimmy had, he found her ability to inspire his thinking and work was a blessing. She was special and he was learning just how spectacular she was.

Ben and Harold were ready when Judge Hackett's clerk opened the court for business on the date set for their motion. The Judge quickly indicated he didn't need opening arguments, the matter having been briefed by both sides, and he proposed hearing the witnesses only and would hear closing arguments when the testimony was complete.

Harold immediately called John Bishop as their first

witness. John's testimony was exactly as he had told them and his account of his mother's cognitive decline over the year and a half before her death was concise and passionate, describing her decline with a catch in his throat. He talked about his monthly visits with his mother and her inability to communicate with him for the better part of a year before her death. He talked about one incident at the beginning of the year before her death when she had briefly recognized him and had tried to write him a note. She seemed unable to speak and wanted to tell him something by writing the note. He broke down as he recounted her shaking hands and the final indignity for her of not being able to write letters or words on her notepaper.

Harold said, "Your witness," and George Faltner began his cross examination.

"Mr. Jones, you are well aware of the value of your mother's property that was foreclosed by the Bank, aren't you?" George began.

"Yes, of course." John replied.

"You also understand setting the foreclosure aside is the only way you can benefit financially, is that not correct?"

"Yes, but I have worried how mother could have been convinced to mortgage her property for such a huge amount that disappeared as it did. I talked with several attorneys but found no one willing to take the Bank on and finally decided it was futile to fight the foreclosure. I got the address of the Bank that deposited mom's check for $950,000.00 and called it to find out who got the money. When they indicated it went to some Ohio company, I followed up and found no telephone number or means of contacting it. I drove to Concordia in Ohio and made a police complaint when the company's address turned out to be a vacant lot. They investigated for a time but finally filed it in their cold case accumulation as another typical scam of many against the elderly.

"I really believe there needs to be a much deeper investigation of the mortgage. Mom was scammed and I believe the Bank was negligent in allowing the scam to work so well against a woman 93 years old and a longtime customer of the Bank. Her loss of cognitive ability was so obvious to me, the Bank should have seen the signs. If the Bank didn't it would be negligence well beyond a simple mistake."

George attacked. "The fact is that you heard about this lawsuit asking for lots and lots of money and jumped at the chance to join and help with this brand-new testimony on your part. It's all about money, isn't it? You're here hoping to win some. It's good old-fashioned greed spinning your words, isn't it?"

John was incensed and it showed. Looking George in the eyes, he angrily responded. "Let's get this straight. We are talking about my mother. I loved her and would never lie for her because she would never stand for it. I don't know what happened to her, but I am here to find out. This case has given us a chance to do what I wanted to do when the Bank foreclosed. David, Sylvia and I share a great love for our mother and want answers to how mom was beaten down to lose the land and her home that she loved so passionately."

"Your witness for redirect." George had no more.

"Thank you, John," Harold began. "I call David Bishop to the stand."

When John left the stand, the look he gave George would keep any normal man from sleeping. It was obvious that the charge of greed rankled and, although John had given it back better than it had been given, he still wanted to hit George.

Ben had been very pleased by such strong testimony and had received congratulations in the form of a subtle pinch from Alice, sitting beside him, that confirmed his pleasure. She knew, just as he did, that John had hit a homerun, and the Bank was going to have to respond or else have her foreclosure stopped.

Harold began: "You are David Jones, a son of Jane Jones, is that correct?"

"Yes, John is my older brother and I have a sister, Sylvia," David confirmed.

"Tell us about your relationship with your mother during the year and a half before her death and tell us what you saw regarding her cognitive abilities during the year before her death."

David: "That period represents when mom began to lose her mental faculties. It began about a year and a half before her death and came to a head about a year before her death when she completely lost her cognitive ability. She was unable to communicate with me or recognize me when I visited her once a month. I don't think she ever recognized me during that last year, and it was hellishly hard to sit with her, holding her hand, and talking about her life while knowing she had no connection with reality. We kids all loved her for being the most generous and loving person in the world. She was also one of the smartest people you will ever meet. That mortgage would never have been put on her land if she had even a small portion of her normal abilities. We want a deeper investigation of that mortgage and what measures, if any, the Bank took to protect her. We believe there was negligence in the failure to recognize her lack of mental capacity to take out a massive mortgage for the first time in her life and then to allow the issuance of a check to someone for the full amount."

"Your witness," Harold said.

"Mr. Jones, I believe you heard my questions to your brother John, and I am going to ask you the same basic question," George began. "Is it not true that you, John, and Sylvia, see this lawsuit as your only chance to get some of your mother's substantial estate and have offered to help by giving this new, obviously coordinated testimony regarding your mother's supposed cognitive failure?"

David responded, "You are correct in part because a positive result in this litigation would mean a substantial financial boost for all three of us, but your fundamental premise that we are here only for the money is wrong and deeply resented by all of us. My intent is much more focused on the factual basis of the Bank's foreclosure and how it relates to its potential negligence. My mother was unable to fight for herself when close to death, but we are here to fight for her. She was not a foolish old woman. She lived her life as a warrior, and we stood in awe of her. She never backed down and we won't either. You impute greed to us. You claim coordination of our testimony. You are flat out wrong. We each visited our mother regularly and saw the complete loss of her faculties."

George was not having much luck and Ben was not surprised when George turned the witness back to Harold. Ben was on his feet immediately to request a short time to consult with his co-counsel. Judge Hacket gave the time routinely and Ben moved away from the Bank's counsel table for privacy. He thought they had presented enough testimony of cognitive decay to force the Bank to respond and should forgo Sylvia's testimony. Harold agreed and advised the court that the Plaintiffs rested.

George had Dex Henderson as his only witness and called him to the stand. After establishing his name and position as President of the local Bank branch, he began his questions.

"Mr. Henderson, did you meet with Mrs. Bishop prior to the day she executed the mortgage your Bank foreclosed?"

"Yes, I did," Dex said. "I met with her on several occasions, and we discussed her account with the Bank and her plans for construction of homes for her children on her property."

"When did you have the meetings you describe?"

"During the year before her death and, in particular, during the last two months of that year."

"You have heard her two sons testify here today, that she was mentally out of it during that period and unable to talk with them or even recognize them. Is their testimony accurate in its description of her mental state during the two months you met with her?"

"It is not. It is plain to me that their interest in winning this ridiculous lawsuit has robbed them of the ability to tell the truth. When I met with her, she was bubbling with her anticipation of the homes' construction and had pictures of homes the company in Ohio had built. She was really taken with large ranch homes with lots of glass for views of the bays and city. She loved her kids, and her plans gave her great pleasure that she shared with me. I think she would be very sad hearing their testimony here today."

George went on with Dex, getting his testimony about a meeting in which he said, "she had told him about Otto Cambridge, the builder from Ohio." He testified: "She told me she believed that Cambridge was the right man to build the homes. She had drawings and pictures of the homes he would build. She said she had a solid purchaser for the portion of her property not used for the home sites for enough to cover the mortgage balance. I saw no reason to question her decisions and assured the loan officers of the Bank that there were no apparent problems with the new mortgage and disbursement of the funds."

Ben was sitting almost in a daze at what was obviously perjury by a man he had counted as a friend before Alice's story about his actions toward her. Ben had been surprised to learn about Dex's refusal to honor his guarantee, but this was so much worse. He had thought Dex was involved in some way, but the perjury opened new worlds of speculation. His testimony was the last straw. It was conclusive to Ben that Henderson was involved up to his eyeballs in the Bank's granting the mortgage to Mrs. Bishop and then allowing her check to be cashed. His mind was racing, and he suddenly realized that the scammer was probably sitting in the witness stand. He also thought this was not the time to raise the issue. If Henderson was the scammer he sure as hell didn't want to scare him into cleaning up whatever mess or materials that might exist to give his identity away. He would let Joe Binds go after it in depth and then act on Joe's findings, if any.

George turned Dex over for Ben's cross examination and he stood directly in front of him and began.

"Were you present when she executed the new mortgage and, if so, did you observe any difficulty on her part in signing her signature on the mortgage?"

"Yes, I was there, and she had no difficulty signing the mortgage. I made sure her signature was checked carefully at the Bank and confirmed as genuine based on a series of checks and documents signed by her over the preceding year. I made sure the transaction was error free because of her advanced age. Our Bank prides itself on attempting to prevent the scamming of our elderly depositors."

"Did the Bank do any checking on the Ohio company

that you have indicated was working with her including a credit check on Otto Cambridge, the owner of Ohio Home Construction?" Ben asked.

"Our check showed the existence of the company and there seemed no reason to do more."

"Was her mortgage reviewed by anyone at the Bank's main office?"

"No, it was not necessary since it was well within our local limits for loan totals."

"No further questions of this witness." Ben concluded.

"I have no further questions and we rest." George added.

Ben addressed the court. "I would appreciate the usual recess at this time to review the testimony," Judge Hacket agreed and said the recess would be for a maximum of thirty minutes.

Ben, Harold, Alice and the Bishops immediately went into one of the attorneys' rooms. Ben and Alice could hardly talk for a moment and then Ben put his conclusions on the table.

"That son of a bitch just perjured himself and the only reason I can see is that he is the scammer who stole Jane's money. I held back on my cross of him because we cannot go after him today. The last thing we should do is force him into trying to clean up whatever evidence we may find through a deep investigation. My investigator is the best in Michigan, and it is obvious Henderson is sure he has covered his tracks perfectly. He couldn't testify the way he did if he thought there was anything out there that could trip him up. He doesn't know Joe Binds, but I do. We will track him down.

We need the checks on her account. We will have them soon enough and not just the signatures she is supposed to have done, but the writing of the names of the recipients will be available for examination and comparison to his handwriting. There are forgeries here that we can have compared to Henderson's writing. He thinks he is untouchable and he's wrong. I will bet up front that Joe will find a witness or two in Ohio who can identify him where that scam company was formed."

Ben continued laying out his suggested approach. He told Harold: "I think our testimony has been sufficient to establish a clear dispute and a basis for the Preliminary Injunction. I think it wise to not present the nurses' testimony since it will tell Henderson we are challenging him directly. We have sufficient evidence before the court for the Injunction we want and, stopping at this point will give Henderson a feeling that his testimony has raised no dangerous issues for him. The bulk of his anger, if he loses on the injunctive relief, will be directed at the Judge, not us. If Judge Hacket rules for the Bank, there will be an opportunity in the future for us to reopen the matter and Dex will be certain in the meantime he will carry the day in the ultimate trial."

It looked like a win-win situation, and Harold agreed completely. He had also been astonished at what they had heard from Henderson. The obvious perjury from the Bank's President was so unexpected it boggled the mind. His reaction was clear enough. He knew at that moment his clients were going to win and get their mother's home and land back. He was elated and shared a handshake with Ben and Alice, thanking them for their decision to take the Bank on in court. One thing was for sure, their discussion had to remain a complete secret during the time of investigation and research. All six in the room agreed the litigation had to proceed in a normal fashion, dawdling a bit in court while waiting for a firm trial date. The investigation had no time limits and could take several months. Ben was committed to paying for it and Harold volunteered to help. They would not ask to speed up the process and Henderson would expect his testimony would be the clincher with a jury.

They went back into the courtroom and, when the Judge gaveled the case into session, Ben said that the Plaintiffs rested and would rely on the testimony presented. Judge Hacket sat back for counsels' argument and Ben began with a simple approach indicating the Plaintiff's belief that they had presented testimony creating a reasonable doubt whether Jane Bishop had been mentally capable of executing the mortgage in question and the Bank's testimony simply created a clear dispute. Ben said, "The obvious dispute in the testimony regarding her capacity supports the Plaintiffs' request for Preliminary Injunctive relief and should justify stopping the foreclosure of Alice's property pending trial."

Georger argued that Henderson's testimony was so clear and dipositive of the Bank's alleged liability there was no basis for preliminary Injunctive relief for the Plaintiffs.

Judge Hacket took only a few minutes to order the Injunctive relief Ben had asked for and the matter was done pending trial. Harold was ebullient and Alice gave Ben a hug and kiss on the cheek. Ben was inordinately pleased, far beyond his legal win.

Perjury

Ben and Alice met with Joe in Ben's office and brought him up to date on the perjury. It was plain enough that Henderson had been involved in the land transactions from the beginning but there was still no indication of who was behind the possible murder of Jimmy. Ben was confident that Dex had forged Jane's signature and probably her checks but there didn't appear to be any connection to Jimmy's murder. Although the Bank had made beaucoup bucks in its foreclosure of Jane Bishop's land, and Henderson had almost certainly been handling the scamming of Jane Bishop, there was still no motive they could see for Jimmy's death.

They discussed the parameters of Joe's new investigation. The Otto Cambridge in Ohio who took Jane's almost one million dollars had never been found or identified by the police. Ben believed the court employees who worked with the mythical Otto would be the best bet for identifying Henderson as the scammer. Although they presumed Dex had been disguised, Joe indicated he would do a projection of Henderson's face with several different beards and various styles of glasses, dark or otherwise for the clerks to look at. They were sure that Henderson's high right eyebrow would give him away. It was so obvious there would be no way to hide it.

"Don't worry, I will pin the bastard," Joe said. "He had to leave tracks and I will find them." Ben agreed and brought up one of the keys to his attack on the Bank. "Although we haven't seen them yet, I believe there were quite a few checks drawn on Jane's account in that last year. Given what we know about her total inability to execute her signature, he must have been living on her money for almost that entire year before her death. He had to forge her signature for an extended time and the Bank should have been concerned about her ability at 93 to continue signing with the same capable strokes. Regardless of mental issues, it is a normal situation for a person's signature to change in obvious ways due to advancing age. If the amount of money drawn from her account was large when added over time, bells should have been ringing loud and clear at the Bank. Failure to act by the Bank would be gross negligence, not to mention the Bank's failure to pick up on its President being the only contact with her and the huge amount of her mortgage."

Ben told him. "Spare no expense and stay on the search for as long as it takes. I want to know what the police have done and what they have in their files. It's been a couple of years and I suspect they would love to nail someone for the scam. Make sure they don't know who we suspect since the last thing we want is the Ohio police telling him he is a suspect."

Joe agreed and they shared a drink in hopes of his anticipated success in finding the evidence Ben needed to nail Dex at trial. "He won't see us coming," Ben said. "I am planning on reaming his ass painfully. I know this is going to take a lot of time so keep us advised on progress."

Ben spent the evening with Alice at the Park Place Hotel's fine restaurant talking about their progress in the case and sharing a new sense of optimism. He was finding his time with her to be so captivating and warm; he thanked his lucky stars that she had come to him for help. Jimmy's recommendation and his many times spent with both at their home had, combined with their working together on her case, set something in motion that was growing more important to him every day. He enjoyed her company tremendously but believed it was far too early to consider expansion of their friendship so soon after Jimmy's death. It grew tougher for him to handle their regular contacts professionally as his feelings grew.

It was almost certain Judge Hacket would be setting a trial date of at least eight or more months in the future since his docket was full. Ben looked forward to the time he would be spending with her working on his trial preparation and thought that doing some fishing would be fun for both and would lighten the mood from the necessary office research.

She was pleased and they spent a number of days on West Bay in his cruiser, trolling for trout and salmon. She was an ardent fisherman and Ben got a kick from watching her intent approach to the rod setup and switching lures to find the best ones. She had not worked with downriggers and found them fascinating and effective for lure presentation at greater depths than she had ever fished in her lake at home in southern Michigan.

She turned out to be a terrific cook when preparing trout for their evening meal and they enjoyed eating together and the small talk that followed. The time of research and preparation moved along inexorably and very pleasantly while they waited for Joe's return.

2nd Investigation

Joe set out to do the intensive investigation Ben had assigned. He started with a series of long-range shots of Dex Henderson, making sure there was no way for Dex to know he was being photographed. With a series of photos, he began adding various styles of beards and glasses to the images, reasoning that some combination would jog the memory of people who had encountered Dex while he was disguised. Using his contacts with the State Police, he got a copy of the Ohio police report on Jane Bishop's scam. The Michigan State Police had relied almost totally on the Ohio police report which contained Jane's mortgage and check information including copies of both. The Ohio police had approached the case assuming the scammer was an Ohio citizen and had been unable to find a perpetrator from the descriptions given by the Bank personnel who had handled his account. They had asked the Michigan State Police to run the description against its extensive database of criminals and the Michigan police were unable to find anyone meeting the description. The Ohio police had put the case in its extensive list of unsolved scams pending any new information.

Joe was interested in the handwriting of the signature and name of the receiver of the mortgage money but knew he needed expert help for the analysis. His buddy from his days with the State Police had been on his mind since Ben had brought him into the case. Jim Blazer had been the best handwriting analyst in Michigan and was still active after his retirement from the State Police. He was working for several companies and Banks where his unique skills were being used to find forgeries and identify those responsible. Joe called him and, after explaining what he wanted, sent him copies of the check and mortgage along with a sample of Dex Henderson's handwriting that he had found in a note from Dex to one of his employees having marital problems. The note had been in the court records of the employee's divorce action and Joe obtained a copy. Jim promised a quick turnaround and Joe set off for Ohio.

The Ohio police report gave him a starting point for his own investigation of the DBA in Concord County. The Ohio police had an identify kit picture their artist had made of the so-called Otto Cambridge from the Concord County Clerk's and the Bank's account manager's description. Joe examined it carefully. The high eyebrow over the right eye was there and Joe knew he had his man. Although it had been a publicized quirk in the search for Otto Cambridge in Ohio, no one had indicated knowledge of his identity. The Ohio police had no one to compare their kit likeness to and the search in Ohio had reached a dead end.

Joe adjusted his images of Henderson to include a beard and dark glasses described to the Ohio police by the County clerk and headed for Concordia. He found a nice motel on the edge of town and got a good night's sleep. It had been a long drive from northern Michigan and rest was welcome. The next day was a dull, cloudy day and he parked a little way from the County office. He had the name of the clerk who had been working when the man known as Otto Cambridge had filed his DBA. The police report gave the clerk's name as Mary Cangon, a woman in her forties, who had worked there for almost twenty years. The police report commented on how angry she had been for having unknowingly assisted in a scam on such a vulnerable old woman. She had taken it as a personal attack, having a mother moving toward old age.

He walked into the office, pleased at its no nonsense layout with clean desktops and a smiling woman rising to meet him. She asked what she could do for him, and he asked for Mary Cangon.

The smiling clerk said, "You have me." Joe introduced himself and told her why he was there. She clapped her hands and told him how pleased she was that the scam was still being investigated. "I want that scumbag caught," she exclaimed. When Joe put the picture of Henderson with his beard and dark glasses on the desk in front of her, she jumped up in excitement. "That's him. That's him. I remember that high eyebrow over his right eye and the facial structure. I've never seen an eyebrow like it. That full beard and dark glasses can't hide his eyebrow. That's Otto Cambridge, for sure. Since you have his picture, I assume you know who this man is, and I hope and pray you get him sooner rather than later. She could have been my mother and the police told me how brutal the scam was. Our police tried so hard to identify him, I was devastated when they couldn't. Please tell me that he will be nailed."

Joe then put a picture of Dex Henderson without a beard or dark glasses on her desk and asked if she had ever seen this man. She said "Yes, of course. That's Otto Cambridge." Joe asked how she could identify the man without the beard and glasses so easily and she just pointed to the high eyebrow and said, "Not only that high eyebrow, but I could also picture that face without a beard, and it was the face you just showed me. Note his haircut. His hair was brown and had an immaculate cut with long, western style sideburns." He asked her to write out her recognition of the man in both photographs as Otto Cambridge, and, when it was done, had her swear to her handwritten statement with a copy of both pictures attached. She told him she was not only ready to testify whenever needed, but wanted to be there when the bastard was convicted. "He used my office to take that poor old woman's money and that's not right. Call when you need me. Here is my personal telephone number." She shook his hand to thank him and to make her bargain complete. He thought of the cases he had been part of and realized she would be a tremendous witness. She would handle cross examination very well and he made that comment in his notes for the final report to Ben.

After his success with Mary, he headed for the Ohio Bank where Otto Cambridge had set up a Bank account to launder his scam money. He found the large Bank building with many customers going in and out. It was the kind of Bank where an individual would not stand out as he would in a small Bank in a small town. Concordia was large enough, and his preference for anonymity would shape Dex's choice. He would have wanted to blend in, and the Bank and town were perfect for hiding in public.

Joe went through the same approach he had with Mary when he met the Bank employee who had deposited the huge check from Jane Bishop. It was obvious Carrie Blasé was just as angry as Mary Cangon had been and that she had done her best to help the Ohio Police when they had been working with her on her description of the so-called

Otto Cambridge. She realized the scammer had completed his scam right in front of her and felt terrible about it. Joe asked to meet with her and her supervisor present as a witness when he showed his Henderson photos.

When the supervisor indicated another employee, Janice White, had initially set up Cambridge's account, Joe asked that she also be there to see the pictures. When all were present in the supervisor's spacious office, he laid his photo of the bearded Henderson on the desk in front of them and asked if they recognized the individual shown.

It was instantaneous. Both Carrie and Janice exclaimed, "That's him."

Carrie said, "Look at that eyebrow, I would recognize that anywhere and the shape of his face. Janice chimed in, "I would know him anywhere. That eyebrow stands out like a beacon but it's not the only thing. His face, regardless of the beard, is all him. I also told the police that he had brown hair that had been cut by an expensive barber and long, western style sideburns. His belt buckle was one of those large, fancy ones like the rodeo cowboys wear and it stood out. He set up that account only a little while before the check came in and Carrie and I were concerned about the size of the check. We called the Bank the check was written on and were assured by its head teller that the check was genuine. We had no basis for refusing to deposit it and have regretted it ever since. The police told us that check was part of a scam against an elderly woman who died at about the same time."

Joe put the clean photo of Henderson without any beard or glasses on the desk. They both responded that he was the same man who had worn the beard and dark glasses. He asked how they could be sure, and both mentioned the high eyebrow and their certainty that the picture of the man clean shaven, was a photo of Otto Cambridge. Joe asked if they would be willing to point that man out as Otto Cambridge in a courtroom and back it up when challenged by the defense. Both said they were ready and anxious to do it. Joe told them he knew who Otto was and that he was working for an attorney who would make sure he would be prosecuted for his crime with their help.

New Report

oe left the Bank walking on air. He knew what Ben could do with the statements and witnesses and that Henderson faced the worst day of his life in the upcoming trial. They had yet to look at the signatures and other samples of handwriting on the checks Ben had requested in Discovery, but he thought Jim would have a field day with those as well. With what he had found, he was sure there would be extensive forgeries.

Ben and Alice were sitting on Alice's deck enjoying the afternoon sunshine and margaritas when Joe parked in the driveway and angled over to them. He was there so much sooner than expected they knew something was up. They rose and put their drinks on the table to greet him, suggesting he might like a margarita with them. Joe readily agreed and Ben went into her kitchen to make it. He and Alice could hardly hold their impatience but waited for Joe to start.

With a cold drink in hand, Joe leaned back in his deck chair and said it plainly. "We have him cold. I have three sworn statements identifying Henderson as the scammer of Jane Bishop. He is Otto Cambridge and there is no way he can beat that charge. He got her money and I bet he had been feasting on her Bank account for up to a year. He must be the forger who drew the checks. His testimony was so brazenly false he must believe he is untraceable, but he is dumber than crap if he thinks his actions were foolproof. So far, he has gotten away with it, but the police had nothing to go with to identify him. They had not heard his perjury to know he must be involved."

Ben chimed in. "Dex's meetings with Jane are the actual times the Bank was advised regarding her lack of capability and its failure to protect her from that point forward is gross negligence. No matter that he was the scammer. He was the Bank's representative, and the Bank will be held to know what he knew. Allowing him to remain as President and the only contact with Jane Bishop will be evidence of the Bank failing to detect his criminal actions over a period of at least a year. Jane was violated and who knows how many others suffered. I believe a jury will be forced to hold the Bank liable and will also award punitive damages in addition to actual losses."

He had just finished when Joe's phone rang, and Jim was on the line. He told Joe he had six markers of comparison and could testify the mortgage and check were drawn by Henderson. Joe told him the trial date had not been set but there would be additional checks for his examination to help confirm his testimony. When Joe hung up the three of them high-fived. They had Dex three ways to Sunday as the old saying goes.

They sat together quietly for a long time, each pondering Henderson's actions that were so callous and brutal to Jane Bishop. Ben finally put it into words. "I intend to jam his actions up his ass, and I am sure Judge Hacket is going to enjoy watching it as well."

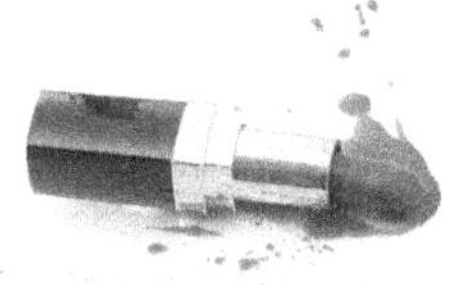

Timetable Adjustment

Dex was in a quandary. He had carried out his original plan perfectly, but Alice was not with him although he still was sure she would be with him eventually. He had to adjust his timetable a bit because of that stupid attorney and began his new plan with the certainty it would succeed, just as the original had put her in financial distress. The fact that a good looking, younger man had stepped in and wormed his way into her affairs was galling but not without an obvious way to eliminate the problem. He knew he had to take Ben out of the picture but had to do it under circumstances that appeared related to some kind of Detroit dispute from his past. He was confident the local businessmen in Traverse City would be looking for some way to point their collective fingers at some dispute far away from the city in the name of tourism and its dollars. There would be no scrutiny at the coincidence of Jimmy's death and Ben's. It had been accepted that Jimmy's death had been accidental and having Ben shot would be obviously not connected in any way. "The locals weren't smart enough to link them" he thought. Sure, it would be a murder but with a motive in Detroit, not this city.

He thought a long time about when he should have it done and decided it should be close to the trial date. That would kill two birds with one stone. Ben would be gone, and the Plaintiffs' trial would be impacted negatively. He was reputed to be the best trial lawyer in town and replacing him would likely be beyond the ability of the fools who had filed their action against his Bank.

Trial Preparation

The copies of **Jane Bishop's** checks drawn during the year before her death, were turned over per Ben's discovery demand. Ben called Joe and they were given to Jim right away. Jim believed he had enough signatures to make his comparison easily proved using the note in Dex's handwriting Joe had furnished him, but he welcomed further examples.

Ben was astonished at the huge amount of money taken from Jane's account over her last year and could think of no reason for the Bank's failure to notice that extraordinary amount. He told Alice: "For a 93-year-old woman with a quarter million in her checking account, to spend more than one hundred fifty thousand dollars in a year should have set off alarm bells so loud they would drown out normal activities in the Bank. "

Harold was certain when he saw the checks that they were final proof of the Bank's gross negligence in the foreclosure of Jane's home and advised her sons and daughter he believed the Bank had no reasonable defense. "We are going to win," he said.

Jim called Ben within two days and confirmed that Dex Henderson had forged her signature on every check and had written the name of the person or company the check was given to. He told Ben, "With the handwriting sample Joe found, I will be able to give expert testimony backed up with so many markers, it will be devastating. When we add the mortgage and mortgage money check forgery, he will have no answer except bluster and more perjury."

Ben and Harold had decided not to depose the Bank's employees, including Dex, believing they had enough firepower without them and planning to bring a level of surprise to Henderson that would give the Bank a terminal headache.

Their premise was supported when George concluded they had little, if anything, more than the two Bishop sons and remained pleased at Dex Henderson's prior testimony. He would defend based on the Plaintiffs' greed and hope for the best. He had been amazed at the amount drawn on Jane Bishop's account when he saw the checks, but it confirmed Dex's account of her cognitive ability and he was bound to defend based on Dex's testimony and the Bank's President's orders. He still wasn't happy at Dex's refusal to consider settlement and hoped his belief that he could handle Ben Bradshaw had more basis than George had observed. He privately thought Dex was in for a skinning and the Bank faced real trouble because of his arrogance. His list of witnesses was short, consisting of Dex, Mary Dobbins, the branch's vice president and Jack Verity, head teller.

Ben and Harold filed their required list of witnesses and finished serving subpoenas on the Bank employees, Dobbins, Verity and Henderson, to make sure they would be available at the trial.

The subject matter each witness would testify to was

not required to be included and George agreed with Dex to disregard their testimony and just cross examine Plaintiffs at trial. He had long ago understood that settlement was impossible and grudgingly had abandoned any thought of that route. He made his preparations for trial and filed the required Discovery witness list.

Love

It had been seven months since Jimmy's funeral and Ben found himself in a position completely foreign to him. During that seven months he had worked closely with Alice on what amounted to almost a daily basis. They had shared all aspects of his preparation including her ideas and thoughts which he found extremely useful and the product of superior intelligence. It had been a gradual process but the result he knew was a deep love for her. She was unlike any woman he had ever known, and he was totally hooked. He knew he couldn't stop loving her and how inappropriate it would appear for him to continue representing her feeling the way he did without full disclosure.

He asked her to meet him for breakfast at the Omelette Shoppe, knowing he could not go on without telling her how he felt. When they had ordered she looked at him quizzically, wondering what the reason for this slight break in their routine was. He reached across the table and took her hand then stopped for a moment while searching for the words he wanted.

"I went home last night and, just as I have for several months, thought of nothing else but you. We have worked together for only seven months since you lost Jimmy, your loving husband, and my best friend. I realize our friendship should be all that is between us on a personal and professional level and what I am about to say is way too sudden, but we have shared our stories and beliefs and my feelings for you have progressed beyond friendship. I have never felt like this toward any woman and am stunned at the effect you have on me. I understand it is way over the line for me as your attorney and I cannot continue representing you without full disclosure. I am violating every rule regarding representation. You should consider hiring another attorney and you have every right to one. You can slap my face if it helps for having worked for you for so long while feeling this way. I know this will appear thoughtless and much too sudden since it is so soon after Jimmy's death. The last thing I want is to hurt you. Even though it is completely out of order for me to say, I cannot stop thinking about you. I have come to love you with all my heart and want to be with you."

She beamed and answered, "You have described how I feel with only one addition. It does not seem too sudden to me. You know that I loved Jimmy very much and his loss was the worst thing I have ever suffered. However, you have taught me I can love another man just as much or more because I have fallen in love with you with my whole heart. I do not care what society believes about how long grieving must go on. How long the time has been after Jimmy's death as a measuring stick is meaningless when my heart, mind and body are speaking in unison. I believe these terrible circumstances have brought us together for a reason. You say you want to be with me and my heart echoes. I want to be with you too."

They shared their first kiss and Ben exclaimed, "I want you in my home. We will set up separate accommodations until we can get married." She looked at him with a big smile and he suddenly realized he had not proposed to her. She laughed at his discomfiture and asked if this was a proposal. He said, "Yes, absolutely. Will you marry me?" Her answer was forceful, "I accept. I will marry you as soon as possible." His response was another lingering kiss and, "Let's elope and tell our families later." She thought that was great. "They won't see this coming," she said, and they laughed together like kids playing hooky.

He said, "I will call Sherry and have her check on whether Indiana still allows marriage without a waiting period and, if so, to find a Justice of the Peace close to Michigan. I know Indiana still has Justices of the Peace that can perform weddings and it should be less than a five-hour drive. We can pack enough for a couple of days and be on the road by noon.

"My good friend Bill has the best jewelry store in town, and I'll call him right now. I am sure he will open for us so I can buy the rings." When Bill immediately agreed, they were at the store before he arrived. The brilliant, diamond engagement ring he slipped on her finger was gorgeous and she was concerned at such an expense. He told her, "Don't worry, I have been saving all my life for this moment." He bought matching gold wedding bands and, after effusive congratulations from Bill, who promised to keep their elopement secret for a week or so, they swung by her home for her to pack. While she was getting ready, he checked with Sherry, who confirmed there was no waiting period in Indiana and gave him the address in Elkhart of the Justice of the Peace she had called. He would be expecting them. When Alice was ready, they stopped at his home for the minimal gear he needed and headed south.

It turned out to be an easy trip to Elkhart with a leisurely lunch along the way. Ben's three-year-old Cadillac was a fabulous road car, and they talked a blue streak all the way, enjoying each other's company and sharing family stories. They had no difficulty finding the Justice of the Peace who had all the documents needed ready for them. The service was performed with his wife and elder daughter as witnesses and they left with their Marriage Certificate in hand, as newly minted spouses.

They celebrated the marriage with unrestrained passion, finding their physical attraction a revelation. They were lovers in every sense. It was late the next morning when, having missed the breakfast provided, they drove to the closest restaurant recommended for a good breakfast. They had no difficulty deciding to stay over until the next day while celebrating their passion again. On the trip home, Ben was over the moon with his wife beside him in the car and their conversation keeping him delightfully awake. She seemed to always know what he was thinking, and they laughed at each other's stories all the way back to Traverse City.

After arrival at Ben's home, he suggested it was time to tell their families the news. "My folks are going to be thrilled. They have been asking when I am going to get around to finding a wife. I think they could never have imagined that I would be able to find such an extraordinary woman to share my life. We are going to get a lot of love on my side, and I hope your folks will be as pleased with me. I sure enjoyed them at your wedding with Jimmy. While you call them, I will hire a mover to bring your things to your new home."

She laughed happily. "My folks are going to be wild for you. My dad has always wanted a son and you fit his bill perfectly." True to expectation, the explosion online was tremendous. They had been worried about her in her period of grief and this was fantastic news. Her dad insisted on talking with his new son-in-law and Ben obliged. It was obvious from the first moments that he was welcomed into their family with the same love he knew she would find in his. They talked for a time and Ben promised to drive down within a week for them to meet him as her husband. She then talked for a long time with her mother and Ben could tell she found wholehearted approval.

It was Ben's turn to tell his folks and the result was the same excited response. His mother talked with Alice for a long time, and it was clear she totally approved and looked forward to meeting and welcoming her into the family. They planned a trip to his folks' New York home as soon as possible after the trial.

Attack

As the trial date came closer, Dex went ahead with his plan to eliminate Ben. He had been appalled and infuriated when he heard they had been married. He screamed in his bedroom that night, "That son of a bitch attorney has to be killed now, not later." He called Ray and asked, "Can I count on you to take care of another guy, a local attorney, who is giving me problems? I don't want this to appear accidental, I want him shot. I should tell you he was an Army Ranger and quick with weapons and I am assuming it will be more than the last one. What's your price?" Ray responded, "I will do it for forty thousand and will keep your identity secret as part of the deal."

Dex was not surprised at the price and readily agreed but he was bummed that Ray knew who he was. They were on a first name basis and Dex realized for the first time Ray could expose him as a partner in Jimmy's murder although he thought it was not all that important since exposure would incriminate Ray as well.

He had come to think of Ray as a fellow killer and, true to form, could not avoid bragging. He told Ray, "Before you killed Jimmy, I finished off a demented old woman named Jane, who owned some land I needed for a deal. I used Abrin for the job. That stuff worked fast, and she was finished within twenty minutes. I got it by burglarizing a drug store more than four hundred miles from here. No way I could be traced."

He expected applause from his "partner," but Ray just saw him as arrogant and foolish. He enjoyed the fact that he knew plenty about Dex, but Dex knew nothing about him. It was laughable that Dex considered them equals in the killing business and Ray chalked it up to Dex's incredible hutzpah which, if it weren't for the money he would earn for this job, he would be happy to do without until his plan for blackmail was ready to begin. He really wanted no part of Henderson. Henderson's moral outlook repulsed him. Killing such an elderly woman was nothing to brag about in Ray's mind since he would never take a contract to kill an elderly woman already in dementia.

He stroked Dex with grudging approval, figuring it was foolish to cut off the money stream, and Dex lapped up what he perceived as praise well deserved, and approved the $40,000 for Ben. Since Dex wanted him shot as opposed to some kind of accidental death and Dex had told him that Ben had been a Ranger, he had asked for quite a bit more than his usual fees.

Dex assumed Alice would be viewed as a victim even more than when Jimmy died in his accident. The press coverage of an apparent execution would be huge, and Dex saw himself as the man who would be her choice for help during her new period of grief. With Ben's killing, his plan would be back on track.

While Dex dreamed about his future with Alice, Ray planned his attack on Ben. He knew a public shooting would bring almost instant police awareness complicating his escape. It was imperative that the killing be in an uncongested area with few, if any, people nearby and clear escape routes with no potential dead ends or pockets difficult to navigate safely. The subdivision where Ben's home was located had major pluses. The residents would be glued to their TVs or sitting on their back decks when he shot Ben. His experience told him they would not recognize the sound of the shots at first and he would have time to walk to his car and drive out of the subdivision without anyone getting close enough for identification. If someone did get that close, he would shoot him or her on the way to his car.

Dex had briefed him regarding Ben's Ranger background while denigrating Ben's intelligence. He described Ben as having wartime experience but a typical soldier's mentality and little in brain power to affect or prevent his killing. He wasn't about to give Ben any credit. Ray didn't care what Dex was thinking and considered Ben's Ranger training unimportant. He believed it wouldn't be a problem even if Ben was armed. His approach would be so sudden, Ben would have no chance to defend himself. His planning for this type of kill was always based on total surprise to the victim leaving no time for reaction, armed or unarmed. He was more concerned with extraneous matters like eliminating any police presence with his site determination and making sure there would be no witnesses close enough to accurately describe him when giving their statements to the police after the event. As always, he would be wearing a disguise.

Ben's wife might be a witness, but her description of an attacker would be based on his changed appearance. Dex had made it plain that she was off limits. Under no circumstance was he to harm her. Ray laughed to himself at that since, if she came close to him, he would clean up the job leaving no witnesses, including her. The half payment of

$20,000 already paid was enough to satisfy him if that came to pass and Dex refused to make payment of the second half. Ray expected substantially more, after both killings of Ben and Jimmy, by way of blackmail. Dex had no idea what he would face in the future from his having directed the murders. Ray was already counting the money in his head as he planned Ben's demise. It was a big, very satisfying number. His blackmail letter was already prepared and stored in his safe deposit box. It included a threat to handle Dex just as he had Jimmy and Ben. Ray never thought of his killings from a moral perspective and just consigned them to job related work rather than murders. Ray was looking forward to fleecing Dex later.

It was about eight in the evening, already quite dark in late October and he was wearing glasses that obscured his eyes but didn't affect his eyesight when he walked up to Ben's door. There were no neighbors around in the plush subdivision that Jimmy had developed as his first success. The next-door neighbor's lights were on, and Ray could hear the TV in their front room. Perfect, he thought. Those sounds might completely muffle the sound of his gun shots.

He rang the doorbell, holding his pistol at his side. Ben opened the door and Ray shot him in the heart and again in the chest with one swift motion. Ben fell backward at the savage blows to his chest and Ray calmly began to turn away, pleased that his job had been completed perfectly. He never saw Ben drawing his Glock as he fell. Ben's first shot into Ray's side turned him back toward Ben and his second shot was alongside his heart. The bullets drove Ray to the ground, leaving him shocked and bleeding heavily from both wounds. Ben's shots had been so fast Ray had no idea what had happened as he fell to the sidewalk, just outside the door. Alice screamed as she came flying down the hallway and threw herself on Ben, certain he had been wounded badly. Ben held her tightly as she sobbed against his chest. He assured her he was all right and helped her up. They walked to the man lying on the walk and kneeled beside him as he looked up with a slight smile, followed by a grimace of pain.

The gunshots had been heard by Ben's neighbor, Jeff Barnes, and he came running to the scene. He joined Ben and Alice, kneeling beside Ray. "It's bad, isn't it?" Ray asked and Ben, looking at the placement of the wounds, said, "Yes." Ray continued, "I am feeling weak, and I know I am dying. I don't blame you, Ranger." He began coughing and his voice got lower, although still understandable. "It was going to happen someday. I was hired by the Banker Dex Henderson to kill you and Jimmy Jones. I stopped Jones on the road and knocked him out before sending him over the edge. That arrogant asshole who hired me bragged he had poisoned a woman named Jane with Abrin to get her land after stealing a hundred fifty thousand from her. He was so proud of himself, he told me how he had stolen the Abrin and kept the rest of it in case he needed to take care of someone else the same way." His speech had been more and more wavering, growing weaker by the moment and his last words before he died were "Kill him."

Jeff Barnes had heard every word, just as Ben and Alice had. Ray's dying statement was so shocking, they had difficulty processing it. Ben spoke first. "Jeff, I want you to write down everything he said and keep it as your memorandum of the dying declaration he made. Show it to me tomorrow and, if we believe we heard anything additional, I may suggest additions from our memory subject entirely to your approval. Please do not tell anyone, even your wife, what you heard here tonight. Obviously, she will have to know some unknown man tried to enter our home and I managed to defend it. That will be on the news tomorrow anyway. What you heard about Henderson must remain secret for your own safety. We will hope he assumes his hired killer died without making any kind of comment and he is home free. If so, there's no way he will believe we know who ordered the attack. He should never know you heard anything or were even here. So, go home. Thanks, from the bottom of my heart, for your courage in coming to help. I am going to call the police and you should not be here when they come since you were not a witness to the shootings and Henderson should never know you were here until we have him safely in court."

Jeff had only one question before leaving. "Hey buddy, it looks like you were shot. How did you survive?" Ben smiled and told him, "Kevlar vests are the rage these days. We have been wearing them since shortly after Jimmy's death because we believed he had been murdered. We had no idea who was involved until we just heard his hired killer name him. Please do not ever tell anyone we are wearing protection." Jeff agreed and left shaking his head in admiration of Ben's anticipation of trouble.

Ben called the police, and they sat in the living room while waiting. Ben told her his opinion that, "A hired murderer's dying declaration won't be enough to make sure Henderson is found guilty. I do not intend to tell what this hired killer told us to the police. We must keep Henderson happy believing we don't know anything. I am going to investigate this new information and we will make sure that Henderson gets his just desserts. He is extremely dangerous, and we must make sure he has no hint of any trouble being tied to him."

Alice grabbed Ben and wouldn't let go for some time. "Thank God for your brain and your ability to defend us.

When I heard those first shots and saw you lying on the floor, I panicked. I knew you must have been hurt and it fractured me. I love you so." He held her quietly for enough time to calm down, astonished that their scamming former friend had killed Jimmy and wanted him dead as well.

The motive that had eluded them for so long came out of the blue for him at that point. "He wants you," he exclaimed. "Nothing else makes sense. He is nuts about you and must think he will get you if he eliminates his competition. Jimmy and I were the only men in his way. He must be crazy enough to believe you will see him as a lover or husband if I am gone. This whole foreclosure action has been aimed at putting you financially in trouble. He must have planned on putting you in such financial straits you would have to turn to him. His offer to take care of you is only explainable if that is his motive. After betraying you with his withdrawal of his guarantee, it would take an incredible delusion to believe you would fall for him. But I'll bet that is what he has been planning for. Jimmy was the first impediment, and I replaced Jimmy as the next one."

Alice was listening in horror. "You mean I am the cause of Jimmy's murder and the attack on you?" "Hell no," Ben grabbed her and assured her it was Dex, not her, who was responsible. "You did nothing but be the most desirable woman I have ever seen, and I am damn glad of it. We are going to get the Bishops' land back and, if Harold and I have any ability at all, a hell of a lot of damages from the Bank while he goes to prison for life with no parole. You always believed Jimmy's death was murder and now we know you were right all along. I thank God for your belief. It led to our wearing protection and saved my life tonight."

Their love making that night was primitive and passionate. Ben's escape from death was celebrated in the best way possible, in each other's arms. She lay with her head on his chest and sobbed uncontrollably for a time. Then she tried her best to kiss away the nasty bruises from the bullets against the Kevlar. He had believed their love making could never be better than their wedding night but had to confess it was better and better all the time. He loved to stroke her body and his thought was, "my God, how can any man be so blessed?" She made sure he knew how safe she felt in his arms and how she needed to hold and touch him in return. She did her best to forget that picture of him lying in the hall at the front door. Her love for him was so incredibly strong she felt they were suspended in their own world when she held him.

The newspaper headlines next day featured Ben fighting off a home invasion with shots exchanged. Ben's Ranger background led the story, and he was pummeled by his friends all day with their admiration and good wishes. The Police Chief held a press conference and addressed a crowd of reporters from all over the state. The duel caught the national news and the first question put to the chief was how badly Ben had been wounded. The answer was brief. "The attacker fired twice but missed because he was impacted by Ben's shots. His attacker met an Army Ranger, and it turned out to be fatal for him. It was a remarkable defense by Ben against a brutal attack clearly aimed at killing him." He paused to tell everyone how much he admired Ben's instantaneous reaction and defense of his home and wife. The reporters' reaction was universal, a chorus of praise for Ben.

Ben listened to the TV press conference and was pleased at the chief's approach. He had donned a new shirt while waiting for the police and made sure the chief understood he wanted no one to know he had been shot and had worn the Kevlar vest that saved his life. He did not want Dex to know he wore protection because he fully expected another attempt to kill him. The Chief argued against Ben's request because of the danger Ben was assuming. "Whoever it is could do it in a lot of ways and there is no way to protect you one hundred per cent of the time," he said. Ben's answer was simple enough. "I don't know who he is or why he wants me dead but am damned if I am going to let him know I am ready for him. This is as personal as it gets, and I intend to beat him." The chief promised secrecy and Ben took his word with a strong handshake between men who knew what life exacts and what real danger is.

Again

Dex was livid as he watched the press conference praising Ben Bradshaw. He raged at what a lucky son of a bitch this dullard was. He stewed about it for half a day and then decided on a new course of action. So, Ben's Ranger background helped him kill Ray, so what. There was time to do the job before the trial, scheduled in ten days. It had become personal in every way with Alice as the prize. He counted on her choosing him with Jimmy and Ben neatly out of the way. "How can she refuse me," he thought. He had concluded that he was every bit as good as Ray at the killing business and began his planning.

There was no way he intended to face Ben at close range since Ben was obviously terrific with a pistol. He finally thought of using a sniper type rifle from long range. He had done a little bird hunting in his teens and had been a good shot. At least his memory told him he was a good shot and he had enjoyed the shooting. He assumed a rifle would be easy to shoot and was sure it would have a telescopic sight to enhance his accuracy.

He spent time online and found a gun show where he could buy the gun he coveted without registration or a background check. The show was in western Ohio, an area he had never visited, and he thought the chance of identification would be so small as to be negligible. He took a vacation day, ostensibly to do a little hiking, and headed for the gun show. The sniper's rifle he found was just what he wanted, and he was able to add lead tipped hunting cartridges as part of the sale. There was no requirement of identification of the buyer.

Arriving home with the rifle, he spent some time online looking for a place where he could check its accuracy. He found a state park featuring a gun range located north of Petoskey and off in the boonies a bit, which fit the bill. He would not be noticed there and was sure he needed only a few shots to confirm he could hit that idiot attorney when he tried. He laughed as he imagined Ben trying to defend himself with a pistol at three hundred yards. When he fired the rifle for the first time, he was surprised at the recoil but after a few shots found the telescopic sight handled his aim effectively. He managed to keep his shots in an eight-inch circle, just right for Ben's heart. He began planning for how and where he would make the shot, needing a spot that had an easy way to leave. He would have to be gone before anyone even started looking for the shooter. Alice, beautiful Alice, would be in his arms for solace soon enough.

He remembered Ray sharing his successful plan for Jimmy and set out to surveil Ben's home for the best time to do the job. He assumed the evening would be the best time since there was a small hill west of their home, and he would have the sun settling behind him. It was certain that there would be a concealed spot at the top of the hill where he could make the shot without anyone seeing him. He planned his approach to the home accordingly. It was exciting to act, and he could see why Ray had seemed to be happy with his work. He dressed for hiking and walked into the small area of state land behind Ben's subdivision, having parked his car a half mile away on a dirt trail that led to a dead end with a turnaround about a mile from Ben's home. He carried the rifle on his back in a soft, dark case that blended with his dark jacket. Soon enough he reached the base of the hill that overlooked Ben's home and began his ascent. It was easy climbing except for the heavy growth of bramble bushes and some fallen trees and their stumps. He managed to catch his left hand on the sharp thorns of a bramble bush and had to move on while dripping blood. His heart was racing, and he cursed his failure to bring some Band-Aids. The bleeding did not stop until well after he had reached the top of the hill and settled down in a spot hidden in the weeds that overlooked Ben's house. He found that he had a perfect view of Ben's deck and could lie without being seen in the tall weeds and undergrowth. It was seven in the evening and, sure enough, Ben and Alice were sitting on the deck with margaritas in hand. He looked through the rifle's telescopic sight and saw that Ben's chair was facing his hiding spot and gave him a perfect line of sight to Ben's chest. He chuckled at the perfection of his view and said, "Goodbye Ben Bradshaw and welcome Alice. You are going to be the grieving widow again and will need my warm embrace and support." He thought, so much for coming back later, this is as good as it will get.

Ben and Alice were sitting on the deck comfortably discussing the upcoming trial. Harold Brown had been a terrific help although stunned by Ben's revelation of Henderson's role in Jimmy's and Jane's deaths. Their witnesses were all going to be in town, sequestered in the Park Place Hotel as members of a party group under an assumed name. He was taking no chance with any interference or possible attack on them. Dex had been quiet and that was a source of concern for Ben and Harold as they prepared for the trial. They knew he was capable of almost anything if he felt threatened and hoped they had managed to keep him thinking he was able to win for the Bank.

Meanwhile, Dex was pondering whether to shoot for the head or body. He was concerned that if he attempted a head shot, he could miss entirely. The round he was using was a hunting bullet designed to mushroom on contact, causing a huge wound as opposed to a military bullet that would probably go right through Ben's body. It was an easy decision since Ben would be dead either way. He aimed at Ben's heart and pulled the trigger.

The rifle blast and the terrific blow to his chest were almost simultaneous and Ben fell backward in his chair to the deck. Alice sprang to cover him with her body and screamed for help. Dex continued to watch for a few moments and, certain that he had nailed Ben with a killing shot to his chest, backed out of his little nest and walked down the hill easily on his way to his car. That's a funeral I will enjoy, he thought. It is proof that some jobs are better done by the boss, not some employee. Full of pride for his professional approach, he drove home with his final plan about finished. "How about that, Ray," he thought. You never believed I was any good, but you are dead and I am not he crowed, in appreciation of the expertise he had demonstrated by his perfectly planned execution of his rival.

Counter Plan

Ben continued to lie on the deck, hoping to ensure no more shots would come. The bullet had hit him solidly in his chest and the Kevlar had, again, saved his life although the blow had been painful as hell and worse than the prior attack. He whispered to Alice, "I am going to play dead. Cover me with that blanket and continue to act as though I am done. If he is still sitting out there, he will be watching, and I want him to think he got me. Give it five minutes and then call the chief and get him here right away. Call Joe. I need him along with someone from the State Police as well as our police chief for a conference. Call Harold and make sure he can be here too. We will need me transported to a funeral home to publicly confirm the fact that I am dead. If no one in the subdivision made the connection with the rifle shot and me, we have a little time to set this up."

"Barney Little has the best funeral service in town. Call him and ask him to come here right away. He is a good friend, smart as hell, and I think he will play this game with us and arrange a fake cremation. Leave me under the blanket. It will get you into the house and safe."

Joe, Sargent Battles, one of Joe's best buddies still active in the State Police, the Chief of Police, Alice, Harold Brown, and Barney Little gathered in Ben's home within thirty minutes of her calls. The recently deceased Ben told them about Dex Henderson and the statement made by the hired killer Ben had killed in the first attack on him.

"I was concerned and convinced the statement of a hired killer wasn't enough to convict Dex and we have been investigating him ever since. Joe has established proofs that he was the man who scammed Jane Bishop, and, if the killer's words were true, murdered her with Abrin. Until she can be exhumed there is no other way to prove she was murdered and, even then, no evidence he did it except for his scam and his opportunity.

I have been planning my cross examination to get him to admit enough for a conviction. When we were told he was the killer's employer and that Jimmy had been killed by his order, it finally hit me that he was fixated on Alice and had been for a long time. I noticed he seemed to get out of sorts at her wedding reception. I think it started there and he has been aiming to have her ever since. It seems obvious now that he planned to Bankrupt her and swoop in as a benefactor who cared for her. There seems to be no other motive and this attempt on my life demonstrates it. He must have been angry as hell when Alice and I married, putting another man in his way."

The policemen were adamant that a criminal investigation had to be started. They agreed Henderson was too dangerous to leave at large and began planning on how they would go after him. Ben jumped in, "If you appear to be interested in him, he will be warned and any evidence in his possession will disappear. I agree that you must begin an investigation of this shooting. Go ahead and check out where he was when he shot me. He must have been on that little hill facing our deck and there's always a chance he left something you can use to identify him. But please stop there.”

“He appears sly enough to protect himself if he gets even a hint we are looking at him. I can pin him on the stand and get him rattled to the point of admitting his attacks on me. You have sufficient facts for search warrants for his home and car that you can serve when we have him tied down in the courtroom as a defense witness. I think you will find that bottle of Abrin and his rifle. I expect the rifle will be in his car. I will get him, and I believe I have the right to finish him. I am, after all, the man who he has tried to kill twice. He believes me dead and when I appear to cross examine him, he will be shocked beyond words. I will upset his balance to the point of losing his grip on reality.”

Joe agreed and added his affirmation “that Ben was the best trial attorney he had ever seen.” Joe’s reputation from his State Police service helped sway the Chief and State Police. Barney chimed in. “It will be easy to have Ben transported to my funeral home and to announce the cremation with a service to be held later.”

Ben added. “Harold will be handling the trial through the opening statement to the jury and presentation of Joe’s witnesses identifying Dex as Otto Cambridge, Jane’s scammer. By the time Harold has entered all his testimony including evidence of Dex’s forgeries, the fact that he scammed Jane Bishop will be established and there will be nowhere for him to hide. I don’t think he will try to run. He will believe he can carry it off. He seems to have a delusion of superiority so strong he actually believes he can’t be found out.”

“If I am wrong and he attempts to leave the courtroom, go ahead and arrest him because he will be running for his life at that point. I believe he will be confident he can have his cake and eat it too. To save his appearance of power and truth, he will have to take the stand and will be forced to avoid apparent perjury by testifying to the same baloney he said at the prior hearing. He will believe his testimony and being President of the bank will carry the day. He will try in every way possible to explain how all the other witnesses are lying for money."

"I will set him up for the dying declaration of his killer. It will be the final straw. I will hammer him with it, and he will crack wide open if I have read him right and I am confident I have. He thinks he is smarter and better than all of us combined and seeing his foolproof scheme dismantled will tear the very fabric of his being. Harold and I will deliver our killer to you ready for his prison clothes."

The police reluctantly agreed but with one caveat. The Chief said, "we will have plainclothes officers in the courtroom without making a show of it. Henderson won't know they are there, but his every move would be monitored. If he moves to leave, we will sure as hell arrest him to prevent his running."

Ben made sure the police agreed they would bring him his Glock in the courtroom each day of the trial. He couldn't carry it in, but they could as part of security and he was sure Dex would find a way to be armed as well. Ben's concern was his suspicion Dex would have a gun hidden on his person having figured a way to get around the scanners. "I need to be able to protect Alice," he said. They reluctantly accepted his demand although they disagreed that Dex could smuggle a gun into the courtroom.

Barney and Joe sat with Ben and Alice while they waited for the ambulance. Ben admitted "he had been worried that Dex would hire someone who would try a head shot. Thank God he was good enough to hit me on the Kevlar." Alice couldn't keep her hands off him and was on the verge of breaking down. "I don't know if I can take any more of this," she said. "Jimmy's death was terrible, but having you shot twice scares me so badly I am unsure I will ever sleep again. I heard what you said about the trial, but it is all speculation. I am scared for you." He reassured her that the end really was coming in the trial, scheduled within less than a week. "I am going to finish him, and you can count on it. We are going to be free of this scourge soon and have the rest of our lives to enjoy together." Barney's van showed up and Ben was transported on a gurney into the van. Subdivision residents rushed to console Alice when they heard that Ben was dead, murdered. Alice carried it off with a show of desperate grief and finally was alone in the home. With Joe. When the phone rang and Ben was on the line, she broke down and there was nothing he could say to help.

When her tears had subsided, he told her, "to pack some clothes for him and then take a room in a motel he had found about an hour away. He would meet her." She packed a suitcase for them both and was there in less than two hours. Ben had parked at the far end of the lot and joined her in a few minutes. She held him close until falling into a deep, dreamless sleep.

She woke up about eight the next morning refreshed and ready for war. She walked over to the motel office to pay for her room for the next six days in advance. The manager had several copies of the Traverse City paper on the table next to the door and she saw the huge headline, "Ben Bradshaw Murdered." The paper had the full story of the shooting and a long article about Ben. She bought a copy and went back to her room to show it to him. The article was so laudatory he was almost canonized. It speculated the murder might be related to his Detroit past where he had been a reformer, and the police were confirming their investigation was aimed in that direction.

Ben laughed delightedly at the story. He had hoped for a story that would give no warning to Henderson and he had it in his hands. Alice kidded him about the praise for him although she concurred with every word. She hung the "Do Not Disturb" sign on the door and headed for home to carry out the plan. She intended to limit who could join her in her grief and would make sure she didn't face Dex Henderson. She was afraid she would be unable to hide her revulsion. Joe had offered to be her doorman to make sure only her closest friends made it in, and he was already standing in the front doorway when she arrived. She gave him a kiss and her thanks. He was proud of Ben and her, fully aware of what she would be going through during the next few days before trial. He asked, "Is Ben all right? That was a nasty blow he took. Kevlar stops the bullet but not the pain and bruising."

She thanked him for asking and indicated Ben was doing fine, resting now but eager to continue planning. "He will be calling Harold on his private line, and they will have the entire trial choreographed within a few days. Harold has been terrific. Ben and he have established a strong friendship while working together. I will not be surprised if they form a firm after this case is finished. This shooting changed their approach, but I think they have it figured out. I can't wait to see Henderson nailed."

Not surprisingly, Dex was one of the first to knock on her door. Only a day had gone by since her husband had been killed and he was sure he would be welcomed with open arms with his offer of assistance in handling her grief. He was offended when Joe answered the door and attempted to brush by him. Joe, not too gently, stopped him in his tracks and, mimicking ignorance, inquired what his name was. When Dex, somewhat blustering, gave it, Joe said, "I am sorry, but Alice has given me a short list of her women friends who will be coming, and the list does not include your name."

Dex puffed up and told Joe in a loud voice, "I am the President of the Bank and have worked closely with Alice. I was a good friend of Ben and am sure she will want me with her. I demand that you immediately tell her I am here to see her."

He plainly expected Joe to do what he ordered and was astonished when Joe told him to leave. "My orders are clear enough. If you are not on the current list, you will have to wait for a few days. As her good friend, you must know how deep her grief is and should support her desire to see only her closest women friends at this tragic time."

"You don't understand, I am the one she needs now, and she is going to tell you that if you just tell her I am here." His last words were to a closed door, and he hoped his grimace of hatred for the ass who had treated him like a nobody was not seen by several women walking up to the door. Realizing he could not make a public scene at this place of grief, he turned and walked down the walk to his car, nodding to the women as he passed and saying how terrible the murder was as though he had been with Alice in her time of grief. On the way to the Bank, he thought "this was only a temporary setback. He would be with Alice in a few days and, with the trial coming up, would have ample opportunities to spend time with her. She would see him on the stand and could not help but be impressed with his winning testimony even though it would sink her ridiculous lawsuit. She would better understand and applaud his stature and desirability. As her new, major source of financial support, he would be the most important man in her life, and she would automatically come to him." He had a momentary thought about her family but assumed his incredible desirability would freeze out any other avenues for support, including family.

Trial

The trial date had finally come, and Plaintiffs were ready. The hill where Dex had perched to shoot Ben had been searched and the exact site where Dex had lay while making the shot was identified and searched. The cartridge shell was found along with several large bloodstains, enough blood to make a DNA match. It was Dex's blood, probably from a scratch in the bramble undergrowth on the hill, and the match was more than enough to arrest Dex for attempted murder. It corroborated the killer's dying declaration, and the Chief wanted to arrest him. Because of Ben's and Joe's reputations, he continued to agree, although very reluctantly, to let Ben and Harold handle Dex in the trial but only until the end. He had Dex's home and car under constant surveillance to make he didn't attempt to run and his officers in the courtroom were armed. Regardless of how the trial came out, Dex would face the full power of the law for murder.

The clerk announced the Judge's entrance to the courtroom with the traditional "Hear Ye, Hear Ye" and Judge Hacket stepped up the stairs to his seat at the Judge's bench. He banged his gavel, called the case to order, and addressed the assembled jurors with the standard explanation of their duties and how the selection process would go.

When the first twelve jurors had been seated, Judge Hacket went through his voir dire and then asked counsel for the parties if they were satisfied with the jury. Harold stated that the jury was acceptable to Plaintiffs and George, counsel for the Bank, stated the jury was acceptable to the Defendant. Judge Hacket immediately asked the clerk to swear in the jury and it was done. Judge Hacket then asked, "Mr. Brown, are you ready to make Plaintiffs' opening statement.

Harold rose and made a motion to sequester all witnesses except the parties and representatives of the parties during testimony of witnesses to insure no influence by prior testimony. George Faltner stood and stated that Defendant Bank concurred.

Judge Hacket immediately ordered all witnesses except those described in the motion to be taken to the witness's room provided by the court and said, "The bailiff shall guard that room to ensure no witness waiting to testify can hear testimony being presented to the jury."

Opening

Harold stood and moved to dead center in front of the jury. He started his statement with an apology.

"I know you all have read about the murder of my co-counsel, Ben Bradshaw. He intended to make this opening statement and there is simply no way I can match his eloquence. He was going to tell you about the incredible testimony we will present of the Bank's gross negligence in the foreclosure of Jane Bishop's home.

Jane Bishop was a depositor in Defendant Bank for more than fifty years and was due an investigation of her cognitive health by more than one individual employee when she executed a mortgage in the amount of $900,000 at the age of 93.

We will support the statement I just made to you by presenting testimony from three women in Ohio who are able to describe the scam of Jane Bishop and give their description of the scammer. That scam took all of Jane's mortgage money. We will show that the scam was easily prevented if Defendant Bank had caused a thorough investigation of Jane's total cognitive decline which the scammer took advantage of.

Following that testimony, we will present the testimony of John Bishop, David Bishop and Sylvia Bishop Turner, the three children of Jane Bishop, who visited their mother during her last year and will tell you of their sadness at observing their mother lose her cognitive facilities completely in that period. They will not be the only credible witnesses of Jane's dementia.

Following up on that series of witnesses, we will present the testimony of Mr. James Blazer, an expert with vast experience in the art of determining forgeries from handwriting comparisons. He will testify that there were forgeries of Jane's signature on her supposed checks leading to the theft of $150,000 from her account in Defendant Bank.

We will call several employees of Defendant Bank to confirm no one in the Bank was concerned about her Bank account being systemically raided. Not one person made even the slightest action to protect a depositor who had used that Bank since its establishment and had maintained an account balance in the amount of a quarter million dollars without having made a single withdrawal of more than a thousand dollars during the years before her last year. Think about that. At the age of 93 she was acting in a manner totally at odds with her prior years and no one thought there was a need to check on what was happening."

We will prove Defendant Bank foreclosed on a mortgage it knew was based on the forgery of Jane Bishop and then sold the fraudulently obtained land to Jimmy and Alice Jones. The Bank's fraud prevented title to be passed to them and they were put in the position of spending five million dollars to build a subdivision on that land. We will prove it was Defendant's intent to ruin them financially and steal their profits from their beautiful subdivision. We will prove the Defendants' greed and their criminal actions taken to steal Jimmy and Alice's profits.

We will ask you to award compensatory damages for Plaintiffs' losses and punitive damages for the Defendants' criminal foreclosures.

Harold stood there for a moment, shaking his head in apparent disbelief, and then moved toward his seat at the Plaintiffs' counsel table. He turned and thanked the jury for their patience with him before sitting down.

Ben, sitting in one of the attorneys' rooms, could hear the argument clearly and knew Harold had nailed it. It would be up to him to handle the murders when he cross examined Dex and they had agreed to save Dex's involvement in the scam as a surprise for the jury and for Dex when Jim testified about the forgeries.

He was thinking of Alice having to sit there with the Bishops. He knew she would be wondering and worrying about how it would all work out and unable to appear happy during her make-believe period of grief. Harold had not told the Bishops about Ben and she was deeply uneasy about what Dex would do when Ben appeared. She knew the police had promised protection in the courtroom, but he was sure she was still worried. One thing was sure. Dex Henderson had given Ben his dream wife despite his evil intentions and Ben intended to give him a lifetime prison sentence in return for Jimmy and Jane.

It was George's turn, and he confidently approached the jury. "Let us start with facts," he said.

"You have heard a ridiculous series of opinions but when we get started with testimony, let us see how these purported witnesses defend their opinions with facts. It is easy to malign and defame the Bank but hardly fair when the testimony's purpose is quite simply greed. We are not talking about penny ante greed. The value of Jane Bishop's land exceeds three million dollars. The Plaintiffs are simply asking that the Bank take the loss and that they get rich in the process.

Greed is the culprit in this ridiculous lawsuit. The Bishop children are taking up your time with their hope to cash in on their mother's money even though she mortgaged her home to build homes for them on her beloved land. Greed disposes of grief in their case.

Greed leads me to Alice Bradshaw. The fact is that she and her deceased husband Jimmy Jones signed their mortgage with the Bank, and she does not contest that. She obviously hopes there will be some incredible stroke of luck that will fulfill her greed for the money she lost from foreclosure of her home and subdivision. Hardly a noble cause. We all feel for her grief at the loss of Jimmy and Ben but that is hardly a basis for a judgment awarding her money the Bank has already loaned her.

"The Plaintiffs have said they will bring a handwriting expert to testify to alleged forgeries in Jane Bishop's account. So-called handwriting experts are a dime a dozen these days and whatever testimony he gives should be treated with a whole lot of salt.

You will hear the testimony of Mr. Henderson who represented the Defendant Bank in its mortgage dealings with Jane Bishop. He will testify to his interactions and conversations with Jane Bishop during the period when her children claim she was unable to carry on those conversations. His testimony will be different in every respect from the children's greed-driven testimony and his reputation in this community makes him a credible witness. Incidentally, there will be no greed in his testimony. He is not seeking any pie in the sky.

I thank you for your attention and look forward to the Plaintiffs' attempts to sell their greed as something else." He sat at his counsel table and the Judge indicated it was time for a lunch recess.

Joe came in to pick up Alice for lunch and they walked out of the courthouse to his car. Dex was just a few steps behind and called to her to stop. She continued into Joe's car and closed the door immediately with the window up. Dex came up to the car and asked her to lower the window. She indicated no. He stood there as they pulled away and thought the next idiot he killed would be Joe. He had a moment of acute rage that the little bastard had given him a hard time at her door and now was keeping her from meeting with him. He thought she would have welcomed him for lunch if that son of a bitch had not intervened.

He headed off to lunch with George and complimented him on his opening. "You told them the facts very well," he said. He was unhappy that he could not participate in the handling of the case but understood he had to rely on George to speak for him until he took the stand and set this whole mess straight. He was sure he had disguised himself well enough in Ohio to prevent identification and looked forward to George's cross examination of the Ohio women regarding the failure of the police to find the scammer from their memory of the scammer's looks. He thought his testimony regarding Jane's comprehension would be strong enough to wipe out the Bishops' testimony that Jane was totally demented. He would be home free.

Plaintiffs' Case

As the afternoon session began, Judge Hacket called on the Plaintiffs to present their case.

Harold called his first witness, John Bishop.

"Did you visit your mother during the last year of her life and, if so, please describe her mental condition as you observed and experienced it?"

"I visited mom every month during the last year of her life and would have visited much more often except that she had lost her mental ability to talk or even recognize me. She couldn't write or use a pen and, after the first week of that year, showed no interest in writing anything. In that first week of the year, she tried to write something to me but couldn't form any words and her writing was bizarre with huge letters out of sequence with much smaller letters having no relationship to those before. It was pitiful and enormously saddening for me because she had been one of the most generous, loving people in the world throughout our lives, as well as one of the smartest women I have ever known. It was awful to see her like that. I could only find the strength to be there once a month. My brother David and sister Sylvia shared similar experiences with me, and we all were blown away by the loss of our mother's mental faculties. She was gone from us, and it was the most difficult year of my life."

"Your witness." Harold said.

"What did you think about her plan to build homes for you on her property?" George Faltner asked.

"I don't know where you came up with that fantasy, but my mother never discussed such a plan before her loss of cognitive ability and sure as hell never was able to converse with me during that last year before her death. I think that idea is a cruel joke intended to sell a lie about my mother. I am angry at your question. I don't know if you know that all three of us own our homes and have no need or desire to have new homes on mom's land. She knew that and would never have considered building homes on land she loved so much when we were already happy in our own homes."

George attacked: "The last appraisal of her land was around three million dollars and you and your brother and sister are suing in the hope you will win that big money, isn't that true?"

John gave him a look that would have withered him if physically applied. "Absolutely wrong. We would not be here except for the scam that robbed our mother. There is no one else to fight for her but us kids, and we are here to fight for the strongest and most loving woman we loved for so many wonderful years."

George came back: "That sounds wonderful, but I ask you why you are telling us this sob story now when you said nothing when the Bank foreclosed on your mother a year or so ago?"

"That's an interesting question. I met with Mary Dobbins, your Vice President of the Bank branch, and asked about the foreclosure. She told me the Bank had paid my mother almost a million dollars on her mortgage and had to foreclose or take that huge loss. I thought the whole mortgage deal smelled and talked with several attorneys about raising questions about it. Every attorney I talked with had no interest in fighting with the Bank on a matter that was speculation at best on my part.

I thought hard and long but realized the last thing I wanted was to have my mother's name bandied about as a weak old woman suffering from dementia who had taken money from the Bank that her kids wanted back. She had been a leader in this community, and I was damned if I was going to change the recognition she deserved for her sixty years of community achievement. I talked with my brother and sister, and we decided to let it go. We were sick at mother having been taken to the point of losing her beloved home but had no reason to suspect the Bank was involved or had failed to take precautions to protect her."

It was obvious that George had failed to break John and he turned him back to Harold for redirect after such a short series of questions. Harold and Ben, who was listening, came to the same conclusion. George had been shaken by John's testimony.

Ben was thrilled at how strong John had been. The jury had heard the first testimony about Jane's dementia and John's testimony seemed very believable. John had hammered the first nail in Dex's position that Jane had been able to comprehend and act on a plan to build homes for her children. Ben knew more nails were coming.

Harold called David Bishop as his next witness. "The bailiff has kept you and the other witnesses in a separate room where you could not hear any of the testimony so far, is that correct?"

"Yes."

"How close was your relationship with your mother?"

"We were very close. I loved her and she loved me. I was her second son and she doted on me a bit. John and Sylvia kidded me a lot but we all loved her so much, there was more than enough love to go around." David said.

"Did you see your mother during the year before her death, and, if you did, please describe her physical and mental condition during those visits."

"During the few months before that last year, she was cheerful and usually recognized me when I visited. I was there several times a month leading up to that last year and at least once a month during the year before her death. She changed drastically at the beginning of that year. She seemed to completely lose her mental faculties and no longer recognized me. She was mentally gone for all purposes. She had difficulty dressing herself and was unable to carry on a conversation. In fact, she didn't utter a sentence in the last six months to me, and it was obvious she was no longer in possession of any cognitive abilities. It was one of the hardest things I have ever endured, sitting with her and knowing she was gone from me. I loved her so much."

"Did she give any indication that she could sign a document of any kind during that last six months?"

"Absolutely not. She could not write her signature and that was true for the entire last year before her death. It is inconceivable to me that anyone could claim she had any comprehension whatsoever during the entire year."

"Your witness." Harold concluded.

George began his cross examination with, "It is interesting that you and John seem to have gotten together in planning your testimony. You did work out the language with John, didn't you?"

"John, Sylvia and I shared our memories of mom and our great sorrow at losing her, both in mind and in body. We joined Alice's lawsuit because we wanted to know more about the scam that took our mother's money and land. We have never coordinated our testimony and have been asked by our attorneys only to tell the truth as to our individual memories of mom. Your question is offensive to me because it implies that we have conspired to give perjured testimony. We have told the truth. Your Mr. Henderson has not. Ask him your question about greed."

"That is a ridiculous response to my question. You are here for the money, and we all know that, isn't that true?"

"Absolutely not. We are here to fight for our mother, one of the bravest, smartest and loving mothers anywhere. This lawsuit is our best chance to find out how she was scammed and who was responsible. The money was my mother's and we have never claimed it. Our fight is for her, and we will see it to the end."

"Why has this fantasy taken so long to develop? You had all kinds of time to fight the Bank's foreclosure of your mother's land when she took the Bank's money to the tune of almost a million dollars and then could not pay it back when the legal time came. Where were you then?"

"I was wondering about the mortgage but, when I inquired at the Bank, its head teller Jack Verity told me the Bank had advanced the full amount of the mortgage money and that my mother had used it all. If I wanted to dispute anything, I would have had to attack my own mother and there is no way that will ever happen. John told me how attorneys had refused to attack the Bank and we kids decided not to impugn our mother's memory with a suit against the Bank. I am here now because of the scam against my mother, not because of the money."

George finished with a repeat of his greed mantra, saying, "greed is a powerful force and I suspect all of us in this courtroom have heard enough greed talking to last a long time. Your witness counsel."

Harold was on his feet as George was turning towards his counsel table seat, objecting to George's cheap shot and the Judge responded in the same vein. He admonished George for his comment and told the jury that the opinion of the attorneys would be allowed in their final arguments, but they had the right and duty to disregard asides and comments by counsel clearly based on opinion and not witness testimony. While the Judge was talking, George was being congratulated with a high five by Dex and there could be no one in the courtroom who did not understand George's lack of concern for the Judge's statement. It was the kind of action most juries react strongly against and a major error by the defense.

Harold called Sylvia Turner to the stand.

"Were you close to your mother, and if you were, please tell us about your contacts with her during the last year before her death?"

"We were very close and, as her only daughter, we shared everything. She was my mentor, my inspiration, and my loving mother. I visited her several times a week during the year before that last year. Before the twelve months before her death, she was loving and laughing with a great sense of humor. She was one of the smartest women it has been my pleasure to know, and she always knew what to say when I was blue. At the beginning of her last year, she had a precipitous decline in her mental abilities and I was astonished how quickly she lost it. She began confusing who I was and for almost all that last year she had no idea who I was. It was devastating for me. She had been so much a part of my life I found it almost impossible to sit with her without crying almost uncontrollably."

"During that last six months, was she able to converse with you or write anything?"

"No. She couldn't talk, and it is a joke to suggest she could sign anything. Her nurses described her condition as a vegetative state and shared our deep concerns. They believed she should be in a facility that could help her. She could not dress herself, and towards the end had great difficulty with her bodily functions. John, David and I agreed with their assessment and found a 24/7 facility for her. We were astonished and grief stricken that she passed suddenly before we could make the move. Her nurses were taken aback at her sudden death since they agreed she was in very good shape physically. They believed she would live for a considerable time without issues. She passed so suddenly we didn't have enough time to move her before she was gone."

Harold said, "Your witness."

George leaped up like a bantam rooster and tried slamming her. "That's a fancy follow-up to your brothers' testimony and obviously a coordinated attack on the Bank. Don't you have enough money already without trying to screw the Bank for more?"

Sylvia almost left her seat in the witness box in her anger. "You are so offensive and wrong -I am ashamed for you." She retorted. "I did not discuss my testimony with my brothers and have no idea what they said when they were here. I do know how much we all loved our mother, and we share a desire to find out who scammed mom and what the Bank did to protect her, if anything."

George's face had turned red during Sylvia's answer, and he seemed to be wordless for a long moment. He finally turned to Harold and said, "Your witness for redirect."

Harold quietly thanked Sylvia for her testimony and called Eva Gantry to the stand. When she was sworn and identified to the jury, he began his questioning.

"First, are you interested in the estate of Jane Bishop in any way? Do you claim any money over and above your salary as a nurse from her or her estate?"

"Certainly not." Eva replied.

"Eva, you were one of the nurses charged with the care of Jane Bishop and I am interested in your evaluation of her mental condition during the year before her death. Please tell us what you observed."

"She totally lost her mental abilities starting at a year before her death. It was a sudden and remarkably very close to complete loss of her faculties. She no longer recognized me although I had been her nurse for several years. She had been a delightful patient. Charming, responsive and with a great sense of humor. I loved working with her. It was disconcerting and painful to watch when she so suddenly shut down. It came on so quickly and was so complete it was shocking. I don't believe I had a conversation with her during that entire year and I observed the same problem with her children. She did not recognize them although they had been steady visitors and clearly loved her."

"You have stated she could not carry on a conversation during that entire year. Did she write notes or letters during that year?"

Eva's answer was strong and direct. "Never. She no longer picked up her pen or pencil and when she used them once right at the beginning of the year, her writing was wild and loopy with very large letters out of sequence with much smaller ones. There was no cohesive message with every word attempted misspelled and out of sequence with the other attempts. It was totally different from her writing in the years before."

"Do you believe she could have signed her signature to a document while in the condition you describe?" Harold asked.

"There is no way she could have done it. If anyone claims she did during that last six to nine months before her death, he or she is lying."

"Your witness." Harold turned her over to George.

"How much are you being paid to testify as you have?" George attacked.

"Nothing. I have told the truth and resent your implication that I would lie after swearing to tell the truth. My profession as a registered nurse would be destroyed if I perjured myself in this court."

"What is your expertise to testify that she could not have signed a document in her supposed condition?"

Eva clearly enjoyed answering. "A master's degree in nursing and twenty-five years of experience. I have never seen a person, in the vegetative state she was in, able to sign anything and my opinion is fact based on my extensive experience working with senior patients."

Completely beaten, George said, "Your witness for redirect."

Harold, pleased with the exchange, said, "Thank you Eva for your willingness to testify in this case and for your care of Jane. I call Sharon Cowles."

Harold established Sharon as the second nurse who cared for Jane Bishop and began his questioning.

"You cared for Jane Bishop during her last years. Please describe Jane's mental condition during that last year before her death."

"I worked for Jane for several years and was completely surprised when her mental abilities plummeted in the beginning of that year before her death. I have seen it happen, but such a complete loss is extremely rare in my experience. It was sudden and complete. One day she was talkative and laughing and the next day she didn't know me. It was hard to process because I had learned to love her and her marvelous sense of humor."

"Was there any improvement in her cognitive ability during the year before her death?

"No. She progressed to a condition where Eva and I were advocating placement in a home that could care for her on a 24-hour basis. She had become totally unable to care for herself. She could not dress herself and, near the end, had little or no control over her bodily functions."

"During the last six months before her death, could she have signed any document knowingly and with a normal signature?"

"Absolutely not. I can testify truthfully that Jane Bishop was incapable of understanding or signing any document during the last six months of her life. Anyone who spent time with her during that period would know that."

Harold thanked her and said, "Your witness."

George tried again to tell the jury that the Plaintiffs had bought or directed her testimony. He asked, "Did you spend time with the attorneys for the Plaintiffs in this case and, if so, were you not told what your testimony should be?"

"I talked briefly with the attorneys but was never asked to testify to anything but the truth, which I have. They did not tell me what to say and I would not be here if they had."

George had nothing more to add in his cross examination and stopped. "Your witness for redirect." It was obvious he knew the accumulated testimony was devastating to his client Bank. Henderson was berating him at his counsel table and obviously wanted a stronger defense.

George was in the throes of realization that defending Dex was going to be difficult at best and potentially devastating to the Bank, his client. He had started out assuming that defending Dex was the best approach but now believed Dex had put the Bank in a desperate position since the testimony from the nurses had established he had been lying about Jane Bishop's abilities. His defense was going to totally rely on his testimony, and it was obvious he faced a huge verdict if Dex thought he could sway the jury with a lie presented in an arrogant manner. The accumulation of what he now believed was truthful testimony from the Plaintiffs' witnesses was getting to him and he realized he needed a miracle to get out of this mess without a catastrophic result.

Ben was listening to the testimony and feeling great as witness after witness put it to the Bank. The scenario he and Harold had agreed on was sliding into place and he was champing at the bit while admiring Harold's easy command of his witnesses with simple questions.

Harold, in the meantime, was prepared to present the first testimony directly linking Henderson to the scam and he expected outrage and multiple objections. He was ready.

He called Mary Cangon to the stand and began with, "Please tell us who you are, who you work for and for how long you have worked there?'

"My name is Mary Cangon and I have been the head clerk in the Concord County Clerk's office in Ohio for twenty-five years. My job consists of providing copies of the transcripts of all county meetings and overseeing elections in Concord County including Federal and State elections. I also oversee the routine work of the office including the issuance of DBAs for new businesses."

"Please tell the jury what a DBA is and how it is issued?"

"The letters stand for Doing Business As and the application requires the name of the new business, the name and signature of the principal owner and his or her address for the proposed business. The certificate does not specify the nature of the business. It only gives information to the public of the business name and who is the responsible party in the business."

"In your capacity as clerk, did you assist a man who filed a DBA for a company named Ohio Home Construction?"

"Yes, I did."

"Do you remember the name given you by the owner of that new business?"

"Yes, I remember he gave me the name Otto Cambridge and signed that name on the application for the certificate."

"Can you describe that man for us?"

"Yes. He was about six feet tall with brown hair, a full beard and dark glasses."

"Do you believe you could identify that man if you saw him again?"

"Yes, absolutely, he had very distinctive features and I could see his face and its shape through the beard. The most notable feature was his right eyebrow that was elevated above his eye to a degree that I had never seen before. It was very high. The other clerks and I talked about it when he left, it was so distinctive. I told the Ohio police about it later when they were investigating a scam they said Otto had committed against an old woman in Michigan, but they were unable to find anyone in Ohio who had that distinctive marking and they just filed the scam away along with so many others against the elderly.

In addition, I noticed he had a really splendid haircut with very low, western style sideburns. That haircut was immaculate, and I thought at the time he must have spent real money to get such great work. There was not a hair out of place and his cap didn't mess it up at all. He was dressed in nondescript jeans, a denim jacket, and had a large western belt buckle like you see on those rodeo riders on TV."

"Have you seen that man since he filed the DBA?"

"I had not seen him until I walked into this courtroom but now, I have." She pointed at Dex and said, "He is sitting at that table only ten feet away. That is Otto Cambridge, the man who scammed that poor old lady out of her money and, I understand now, her land."

Dex leaped out of his chair screaming, "Liar, Liar" and there was chaos for a moment. Judge Hackett banged his gavel several times and ordered Dex to sit down and be quiet. He told George to control his client immediately, saying that any such conduct in the future would be dealt with through a contempt of court finding and potential restraint or jailing.

Dex was appalled at the fact he had forgotten about his eyebrow and, for the first time, thought there might be real problems for him. He shook off the feeling with the thought that he could convince the jury with his incredible intellect and obvious power.

When the courtroom had calmed down a bit, Harold said, "Let the record show that she is pointing at Mr. Henderson, President of the Defendant Bank's branch in Traverse City." George stood up to object, but Judge Hacket could see no reason to question the statement which everyone in the court believed was true and told George he would have his opportunity to cross examine.

"Your witness." Harold finished.

George began his cross examination with, "I understand this Otto Cambridge was bearded and wearing dark glasses. How are you sure today that you can identify him as my client when the Ohio Police had your description and were unable to identify anyone?"

"I can't speak for the Ohio Police, but I can speak for myself and there is absolutely no question in my mind that the man you say is your client, is Otto Cambridge."

"When did you first make this so-called identification of Mr. Henderson?"

"When I met Mr. Joe Binds. Mr. Binds identified himself as a private investigator who was retained by the attorney for a client taking action against the Bank where the scammed women had been a depositor. He was respectful and told me not to make any identification unless sure. I told him I would not make any identification unless there was no question in my mind. He then showed me a photograph of a man and asked if it resembled anyone I had seen. I was dumbfounded that he had a photo of the man I understood had scammed that poor old woman. It was a perfect likeness of the man who had filed the DBA under the name of Otto Cambridge. The main item of identification was the eyebrow so high above his right eye, but the shape of his face was a dead ringer for Otto. That photo turned out to be a photo of your client and I was asked to be a witness in this case for the purpose of testifying to my identification of his photo."

"So, Mr. Joe Binds got you to identify my client from a photo he claimed to be of my client, and that is the basis for your testimony, is that not right?"

"No, that is not right. Mr. Binds made no claim before or during my look at that photo. My original identification was from a photo of your client, but I am here now, and I identify him as Otto Cambridge here and not from a photo. I am looking at him sitting there, and he is Otto Cambridge."

"What it comes down to is a raised eyebrow. Do you

actually believe that, because you may have not seen something like this, it does not exist in many other men?"

"I suppose that is possible, but my identification is not solely based on that eyebrow. Look at that haircut with his long, western style, sideburns. When he stood up I noticed a large, western style buckle. I told the police about it and they said there were so many around, it would be no help, but, I just saw your client's belt buckle and there it is on his belt. I can't swear it is the same buckle Otto wore when I met him in my office, but it is large, just like the one Otto wore. If he really is your client, you are representing the scammer who the Ohio police told me stole more than a million dollars from a woman in her nineties who had dementia."

The courtroom had been silent as she testified and her last statement brought a collective sigh in the courtroom loud enough to stop George from talking for a pause, making it even more damning. The jury had joined in that sigh, transfixed by the drama before it and looking as one at Dex Henderson with such a strong sense of anger it took Harold's breath away. He knew this was the kind of moment in a trial when the jury makes its decision and there was no question in his mind that the decision was for the Plaintiffs. George had known it too. He passed the witness back to Harold who thanked Mary with a handshake as she left the stand. The jury gave her smiles as well and Mary sat down behind the Plaintiffs' area happy that she had a chance to nail that crummy bastard. She felt she had helped right a wrong that had been a thorn in her side ever since he had used her as part of his scam.

"I call Janice White to the stand." Harold announced.

"Ms. White, I hope you will allow me to call you Janice." She nodded yes and he continued. "As account manager for Concordia's National Bank, did you establish a checking account for an individual named Otto Cambridge?"

"Yes. He came into the Bank on a sunny day with a heavy beard and dark glasses and I took his details to set up his account for Ohio Home Construction, located in Concord County."

"You have indicated his appearance as bearded and with dark glasses. Did he have any distinguishing features?"

"Yes. He had brown hair cut in a precise cut that was evidence of a very good barber. His sideburns were in a western style, longer than usual, and I thought at the time he ought to be wearing a ten-gallon hat. Aside from the haircut, he had one of the most noticeable facial features I had ever seen. His right eyebrow was raised well above the normal brow line."

"Have you seen that individual since he set up that account?"

"Yes. He is sitting right there, and she pointed at Dex Henderson. That is the man who claimed to be Otto Cambridge at the time when he set up that account. You can see his haircut just as I described it and look at that big, western style buckle, just like the one Otto wore. Finally, look at that eyebrow well above his right eye. There is no question in my mind. He is Otto Cambridge."

The courtroom erupted with anger and Judge Hacket gaveled it into silence. "I will not allow this courtroom to be treated like a circus."

His statement silenced the crowd but had no effect on the collective sense of anger at Dex Henderson, who sat smiling easily in his chair. He had decided to maintain his nice guy look and wait for his time as a witness to handle all this baloney, as he saw it. Still sure of himself and his marvelous abilities, he looked forward to his time on the stand.

Harold knew when to stop. After making sure the record included her identification of Henderson he stopped. Mary and Janice had demolished Henderson and he wanted George to finish the job. "Your witness," he said.

George tried. "Who first contacted you for an identification of this Otto Cambridge?"

"I was asked by the Ohio State Police about who had set up the Ohio Home Construction account and whether I could identify him."

"Were you able at that time to identify Otto Cambridge?"

"I didn't know him, having never seen him before we set up his account, but I gave the police a detailed description of him, including every feature I have testified to here."

"I find this description rather inconceivable since the testimony so far has described a heavy beard and dark glasses. How are you now so certain in your identification of my client?"

"As I said, the haircut, the high eyebrow and the western buckle are definitive as well as the shape of his face. The beard was intended to hide his features, but the shape of his face was clear enough as well as his haircut. He stands out across the board. I have not heard the testimony so far and have not been told he might be here. Seeing him here is a huge surprise. I am absolutely sure he is Otto Cambridge, the man who removed the money from that account in our Bank."

"Your witness for redirect." George finished.

Her testimony was another smashing win for the Plaintiffs. Harold was sure there was no one in the courtroom who didn't believe Henderson was Otto, "the scammer," including George who appeared to be reeling, almost falling. It was incredible that Dex was still sitting with a smile on his face, sending a message to the room to wait and see.

Harold called Carrie Blasé to the stand and her testimony conformed substantially with Janice White's testimony including the identification of Dex in the courtroom.

George had heard enough and thought continuing to cross these witnesses was a losing cause. He said no questions while Dex fumed beside him. Ben, listening, thought the nails for the coffin were multiplying.

Handwriting

The identifications had been terrific, and Harold followed up, calling James Blazer to the stand.

"I offer the testimony of this witness as an expert in the field of handwriting analysis and, if Attorney Faltner wants to question him on his qualifications, he may proceed without objection." Harold stated.

George indicated he wanted to do so, and the court directed him to proceed.

"Mr. Blazer, please tell me your background, educational training and work experience in the field of handwriting analysis."

"I have a master's degree from the University of Michigan in the field of forensic science regarding questioned documents which led to twenty-five years' experience in the Michigan State Police primarily focused on cases involving alleged forgery and identification of individuals alleged to have committed crimes. After retirement from the State Police, I have worked as a consultant for various police agencies and a number of Banks in Michigan. Although my major experience was in the field of law enforcement, I have worked for Defendants in criminal cases to demonstrate their innocence of the charges alleged."

George conceded the witness's qualifications as an expert witness able to testify to his conclusions.

Harold began. "Jim, I have furnished you copies of all the checks cashed on Jane Bishop's Bank account in the Defendant Bank in the year before her death along with an extended sample of handwriting for your analysis. I have also furnished you a copy of Jane Bishop's last mortgage and the check drawn in Ohio by Otto Cambridge. Have you come to any conclusions and, if so, please tell us what you found and the process that led to your conclusion."

"My conclusion is that the purported signature of Jane Bishop on all of those checks and the mortgage were forgeries by a single individual. It was an easy conclusion because the individual forger has several little twists in his handwriting that are impossible to hide because they show up in so many words. I brought a projector to show the jury how I came to that conclusion."

When the projector and screen were ready, Jim began his presentation with a short statement on the differences between a lay person's examination and what the expert looks for. He said, "Trained examiners evaluate handwriting features including the size and slope of the writing, pen pressure, pen lifts, the spacing between words and letters, the position of the writing on the baseline, height relationships, beginning and ending strokes, and line quality. A writer's identity is established through a combination of the significant features found consistently throughout a collection of writing samples."

Standing by the screen with his pointer he first put the sample of Dex's handwriting on the screen without showing Dex's signature on the note. "My first example of the forger's idiosyncrasies that stands out is the way his "e" loops in a counterclockwise direction almost as though he once considered a change but never accomplished it. You can see in the many "e's how that same loop is there for all of them. A similar different way to write r, t, s, w, and n, shows up along with several unusual differences in the height of some letters."

He began to illustrate the items he had referenced, highlighting each letter's shape that he had noted. After showing those idiosyncrasies he then put a series of the checks drawn on Jane's account on the screen and pointed out those same letters with the same unusual shapes and height.

His final slide showed Jane's mortgage and the check drawn on her account for $950,000. The jury had watched Jim's presentation with intense interest and every one of them showed body language indicating their understanding that these were indeed forgeries. The handwriting of the forger, with its noted unusual letters, had been clearly shown in comparison with the checks supposedly written by Jane Bishop. The checks drawn on her account during the year preceding her death showed the same idiosyncrasies and they sat back in their chairs, obviously satisfied.

Jim continued. "I have shown you the sample of the forger's handwriting using the note you saw at the beginning of my testimony. I now show you the signature of the forger on that note. All of those forgeries were committed by Defendant Dex Henderson and here is his signature to prove it."

The courtroom sat stunned at the revelation. The jury sat forward in their seats and their anger at Dex when Jim presented his signature was intense enough to be easily seen. Dex had lost some of his smile at this point.

"Your witness, Mr. Faltner." Harold concluded.

George had watched Jim's testimony just as intently and was in a state of chagrin at the effectiveness and result. He knew there was nothing he could gain by cross examining

Jim and elected to not exam him. Dex's testimony had not a chance in hell of winning. In fact, he had come to the realization that the arrogance of Dex was going to inflame the jury even more than it was right now. He sat in total depression and made the decision that he would not object to the Plaintiffs' case in future testimony. His sense of ethics demanded it. His witness Dex Henderson was a perjurer and criminal scammer. He knew it now as a certainty and was confident the jury knew it. He knew his case was lost. "No questions" he said. Dex was on his feet enraged. "I fire my attorney," he said.

"I am going to represent myself and the bank and I assure you Plaintiffs' witnesses will be questioned in the future."

The courtroom seemed frozen, without motion or sound for a moment before Judge Hacket spoke.

"Mr. Henderson, you have the right to represent yourself before this court but, without corroboration by Defendant Bank, you cannot represent it. I will permit you to represent yourself but will continue to recognize Mr. Faltner as the bank's attorney for all proceedings until told otherwise by a qualified representative of the bank."

"That's fine with me," Dex said. "I have no questions of this bought and paid for so called dime a dozen expert."

I call Mary Dobbins to the stand." Harold said.

After establishing her name, address, and position as Vice President of the Defendant Bank branch in the city, he began his questioning.

"As part of your responsibilities at the Bank, do you handle mortgages?

"Yes."

"Was Jane Bishop's mortgage approval in line with the main Bank's policies as to the amount your branch Bank has authority to handle without main Bank approval?"

"Yes."

"In the last three or four years, have the main Bank's limits remained the same regarding your branch's ability to approve a mortgage without the main Bank's approval?"

"Yes."

"So, there would have been no point where her mortgage would be automatically reviewed, is that correct?" Harold asked.

"Yes, that's right." Mary replied.

"Did you know Jane Bishop, a depositor in your Bank?"

"Yes. I have known her for at least five years and enjoyed her a great deal. She was a bright, lovely woman I considered a friend."

"Was she a frequent visitor at the Bank?

"I would not say frequent, but, for most of that five years, except for the last year before her death, she came in on a regular basis to check her account. She was a perfectionist when it came to knowing every dime she had on deposit even though she maintained a very large balance in her checking account. When I suggested some of that could be drawing interest in a savings account, she laughed and said, at her age, she wasn't interested in the interest, just in having her funds available for withdrawal quickly when the next Banking collapse happened. It was her regular joke and we both laughed."

"Did she continue her practice of coming into the Bank during that last year before her death?"

"No, she didn't, and I tried calling her a couple of times but never got through to her. I worried about her but, when I mentioned it to Mr. Henderson, he assured me she was doing fine, and he had met with her at her home on several occasions. I looked at her account and noticed she had withdrawn a large part of her account with a number of checks. I looked at copies of her checks and her signature was fine and strong. Mr. Henderson's assurance satisfied me, and I just assumed she had some project she was working on."

"After that look at her account and checks, did you make any further attempt to follow up or make contact with her?"

"No."

"You have been in the Banking business for a number of years, is that correct?"

"Yes, I have worked for Banks for fifteen years and for our Bank branch for five years, the last three as its Vice President."

"During your Banking experience, have you taken courses in the ways for your Bank to detect forgeries?"

"Yes, of course. It is one of the important jobs we must perform to protect the Bank and our depositors."

"I have spent some time looking at various curriculums for Banking courses and have found several places in those courses where the change in a depositor's signature is noted as one of the most important indicators of trouble. Did the courses you took emphasize that area of investigation?" Harold asked.

"Yes. That is one of the most important tools in ferreting out forgeries."

"Those same courses I looked at also talked about the normal progression of change in the signatures of the elderly and I wonder if that is also one of the areas you studied?"

"Yes. It is one of the things we look for regularly."

"Did that natural, expected progression of change occur in Jane Bishop's case?"

"Not that I am aware of."

"Since your Banking experience and education say that you should expect change in Jane Bishop's signature, please tell me why her continued perfect signature as she aged into her nineties, did not cause alarm bells to go off."

"I have no valid explanation. I guess it failed to cross my mind although I agree that it should have been spotted in the regular course of our review of her account."

Harold followed. "This 93-year-old woman you liked and who had been a large depositor in your Bank, applied for a mortgage in the amount of $900,000 and the application had a signature that purported to be hers and was virtually indistinguishable from her signatures during the entire period of her association with your Bank. To compound the strangeness of the transaction, she did not come to the bank to confirm such an unusually large debt when compared with her prior practice of precise shepherding of her account. There seems no rational reason why that set of circumstances did not cry out for investigation. A natural progression of change in her signature was expected from advancing age and we agree that was a key marker in determining forgery according to the courses you attended, is that not correct?"

Mary: "When you put it like that, I cannot agree with you more. We should have caught the notable strangeness of her signature showing no change over the last five years of her life, given her advanced age. I feel terrible about it. Mr. Henderson was handling the transaction and I think we slipped up badly by relying on just one person, even though he is our President. The very least we should have required would have been a joint determination by our head teller, Jack Verity, and me, whether we were dealing with a forgery. Our President could have been deceived and we needed to ensure Jane was all right and had signed that mortgage."

"Thank you, Mary. Your testimony clearly shows you

were Jane Bishop's friend, and the Plaintiffs thank you on her behalf. Your witness, Mr. Faltner."

George began. "It is a strong policy of the Bank to look out for its depositors and to protect the elderly, is it not?"

"Yes. We do our best."

"That policy was put in place by Mr. Henderson, your President, was it not?"

"He has reiterated it, but it has been our Banking policy by main office directive for years."

"You and your staff made every reasonable effort to do just that for Jane Bishop, is that not true?"

"I would like to be able to say yes but have already testified that I believe we failed Jane Bishop badly by not making every reasonable effort. I regret so much that I did not react to protect her from what should have been a discovery of inconsistencies in her signature. Our Bank can take no credit for its stated policy when it failed to question her situation more strongly."

"Your Bank President, Mr. Henderson advised you everything was just fine with Jane, didn't he? You had his approval of the mortgage transaction. Wasn't that enough to satisfy any concerns the Bank might have regarding a possible forgery and to meet the requirement for every reasonable effort by the Bank?"

"I believe Mr. Henderson was deceived in some way. This litigation and my understanding that Jane Bishop was scammed put that mortgage transaction in a whole new light and there is no way I can testify we did our job to protect her. We need to admit our failure and make it right for her children. I will never accept being linked to a million-dollar scam by our mistakes without making it right."

"Your witness for redirect." George finished.

Harold had intended to put Jack Verity, the head teller,

on the stand but Mary Dobbins had spelled out the Bank's negligence so perfectly, he decided to forego that and called Alice to the stand. She was sitting as a Plaintiff at the counsel table and slowly rose and walked to the witness chair. Having been sworn in, she sat down and faced Harold and the jury.

"Alice, I understand this is a difficult time for you and. If I could forego your testimony, I would. However, we need to understand your and your former husband Jimmy's dealings with the Defendant Bank."

"Of course," Alice said.

"Were you and Jimmy Jones married at the time you both signed a mortgage with the Defendant Bank for development of a subdivision in this city two years ago?"

"Yes."

"What was the face amount of that mortgage and the reason it was executed by you and Jimmy?"

"It was a line of credit mortgage agreed upon with Mr. Henderson, the Bank's President, for the specific purpose of paying for purchase of the Bishop land and home for one million, nine hundred thousand dollars from the Bank and the additional money required for our development of a subdivision on that land. Mr. Henderson was the prime mover for the deal, having offered us all the funds needed for the purchase and development. He said the Bank required our home to be added to the collateral for the loan and gave us his personal guarantee that he would protect our home. The terms he offered for the mortgage, plus his personal guarantee as one of Jimmy's good friends, made the deal so attractive we agreed to take on at least five million in debt. We put a lot of faith in Mr. Henderson's guarantee and assurances of continued Bank support and would never have gone ahead without them."

"I know this is painful. What happened with that mortgage?"

"My husband, Jimmy, died in a crash on his way home one evening and his death gave an excuse to the Bank to foreclose our mortgage within thirty days of his death. It was one of the most heinous actions I have ever heard of, and Mr. Henderson betrayed us royally. He knew his guarantee was verbal and unenforceable. His apparent plan to destroy us financially, while making millions for the Bank, was confirmed when he refused to give me time to finish a few odds and ends on the subdivision and find alternative financing so I could sell it for the profits we had worked for and the money needed to pay off the Bank's mortgage. He told me a lie that the main Bank had changed the rules. We had completed more than ninety five percent of the subdivision and its value included at least eight million in profit for us within six months or so, over and above the money owed the Bank. Foreclosure would net the Bank much more than double its mortgage investment and leave me penniless in the bargain. It seemed the Bank wasn't interested in my paying the mortgage off when such tremendous profits would come to the Bank with its foreclosure of my land.

Incredibly, Mr. Henderson persistently approached me as a supposed friend wanting to assuage my grief and, as he said, to care for me because of the loss of my home and property."

"You have indicated you believe there was a plan on Mr. Henderson's part. What are you referring to?"

"I believe Mr. Henderson proposed the sale of Jane Bishop's magnificent property intending to allow us to develop it to a point of obvious profit potential, and then, forcing a foreclosure netting the Bank an obscene profit on its loan. If you look at the timeline it becomes clear how the plan worked, and Jimmy's death came at an extraordinarily perfect time for the Bank to complete the plan. It was in place and working well without his terrible crash, but the Bank took immediate advantage by beginning foreclosure within thirty days of his death."

"What financial loss did you sustain?"

Alice took a moment to gather her thoughts and then answered. "It is now certain that the Bank did not have good title to the Bishop land it sold us. I currently owe the Bank five million dollars in repayment of the funds we used to buy the land and pay our contractors for their work on the subdivision. That five million should be added to my loss of the eight million in profits from that gorgeous subdivision Jimmy and I built. I have come to the conclusion Jimmy and I were conned into buying land without good title and to spend five million dollars on land which it appears we never owned. We spent the money on contractors, materials and incidentals required for development of that subdivision on land the Bank appears to have no title to. Our subdivision sits on land owned by someone else and we have no legal claim on it. Our profits from it are lost and gone forever as are the five million in costs for construction and purchase. I did the books for us, and it is absolutely certain our lots were premium and reasonably valued to provide a profit from sales of lots exceeding eight million dollars. It is obvious to me that our loan and mortgage were based on a deliberate plan to Bankrupt us and is the Bank's problem, not mine. I therefore claim compensatory damages of thirteen million dollars. That claim does not include the damage to my reputation from the improper foreclosure of my land based on a public claim that I had defaulted on my loan to the Bank."

"Thank you, Alice. The depth of Mr. Henderson's machinations has been laid out before this jury and I am confident your testimony has given additional context to his sordid story. Your witness, Mr. Faltner, and Mr. Henderson."

"Ms. Bradshaw, do you really believe Mr. Henderson conjured up this years' long alleged plan that required so many variables to come to the conclusion you now are blaming him for?" George began.

"Yes. I do believe he did and his advances to me after his betrayal were unseemly at best. He is a pompous ass, and I would never believe a word he spoke again. So far as allowing him to care for me, I would prefer a rattlesnake for company."

"You assume much when you assert that Jane Bishop's foreclosure was improper in any way. This jury has not heard Mr. Henderson's testimony and this trial is not complete, despite your assumptions. You have already told us you believe he betrayed you. Isn't your anger at him directing your testimony?"

"It is true that I am deeply angered at his actions. I deny however, that I have stated any facts incorrectly."

"No further questions for the bank. Your witness for redirect." George moved to his counsel's table, feeling as though the roof was falling in." Dex rose and walked forward to a spot only a few feet in front of Alice and began. "Mrs. Bradshaw, will you tell us whether I ever made physical advances to you."

"You never did Mr. Henderson. You attempted at times to give me little hugs and tearful statements that you shared my grief. It was the continuation of those many attempts to tell me how much you grieved with me and the multiple times you came to my home uninvited in the evening, which made me queasy and deeply concerned at your motive. Your expression of friendship with Jimmy was obviously false since you had never come to our home before his death and had never sought him out for joint activities. Your numerous suggestions that I would live with you in your home and that you would care for me were astonishing to me, having just lost my second husband in a year to violent deaths. The idea that I was a woman in need of your help was demeaning to me and my abilities to take care of myself. It was incredible that you would think I would turn my back on my family to stay with you. I began to question what your plans for me entailed and there was no answer that made normal sense to me. All I knew was that I wanted nothing to do with you the harder you pushed. You are an abomination, a crude and vicious person who attempted to take advantage of my grief. The testimony about how you took advantage of Jane Bishop to obtain the land you fraudulently sold Jimmy and me is a compendium of actions no honest man could take. All I see is your lies and deception. I would never be with you."

Dex was more angry than ever before. "So, my acts of kindness and gentlemanly concern were your initial basis for concern. Now you have believed the lies from those lying witnesses. I am shocked that you could misread my motives so completely. No further questions."

Harold asked the court for recess to review his notes before proceeding and Judge Hacket seemed relieved at having a few minutes off the bench. He called a recess. Harold and Alice walked into the attorney's room where Ben had been listening. Ben got a terrific hug from Alice and shook Harold's hand with emphasis. "You did a hell of a job. You nailed him and got their Vice President to admit negligence. I cannot imagine anyone handling the testimony better.

I don't think we need to call our appraisers regarding the subdivision values. Alice has nailed that. What do you think Harold?"

Harold echoed the thought. "We have the jury on our side at this point and don't need to give the defense any opportunity to make points on a cross examination."

Ben wrapped it up. "I think George will call Henderson as his only witness. Dex must be champing at the bit to tell the world those witnesses are wrong. He is an arrogant ass; he will want his day in the sun. He also knows he isn't going to get Alice if he doesn't clear this all up and I bet he is still delusionary, thinking his plan will work to get her." Harold saw Ben's grim features and would have pitied Dex if he didn't understand the basis for Ben's demeanor. Harold agreed and they decided to rest their case and wait for Dex to walk into their planned trap.

When Judge Hacket returned to the bench, Harold did the honors. "The Plaintiffs rest," he said. He turned to see Dex Henderson rising to his feet. Here was that good fellow and friend to everyone thinking he could carry the day. "Good," he thought, "here we go, and I look forward to Ben smashing that arrogance out of you. I think your arrogance is going to be a smelly mess in your pants before this day is done. I look forward to it."

Dex Direct

George announced emphatically, "The defense calls Defendant Mr. Henderson, President of the Traverse City branch of the Third Michigan Bank and Trust, the Defendant Bank."

Dex walked rapidly to the witness chair and raised his hand to be sworn. He then leaned back into the witness chair and smiled his "good guy" smile for the jury, all of whom were leaning a bit forward to make sure they heard everything he had to say in response to the testimony naming him as Jane Bishop's scammer. After all that testimony, only Dex Henderson would have the hutzpah to think he would win out and, of course, he assumed his incredible abilities would put the Plaintiffs in their proper place. As losers.

"Mr. Henderson," George began, "Did you know Jane Bishop, and did you oversee her application for a mortgage just before her death?"

"Yes. I knew her very well, apparently much better than her greedy children who filed this ridiculous lawsuit. She was a wonderful older woman, and we shared several laughs and discussions about what she wanted to do with that mortgage money. She told me, and confirmed it with correspondence and pictures, that she had decided to make a final gift to her children of homes on the property she loved so passionately. She had a green folder including all of that and I find it interesting that none of the witnesses who perjured themselves on the stand had the courage to bring that folder to court. The failure of those nurses to share it with you, the jury, is proof they are working with the children as partners to scam the Bank. They understood it would blow their case into the air where it should be."

"Did you have discussions with Jane Bishop within the last month of her life?

"Yes. I have already testified in a preliminary hearing before this court that I had several extended conversations with her during the last six months of her life and found her in full possession of her mental faculties. She had no difficulty signing the mortgage and check to the Ohio Construction Company for construction of those beautiful homes. The idea that all elderly folks have progressive changes in their signatures is laughable since we have seniors reaching one hundred or more these days and maintaining their full abilities to handle their business and continue to sign their documents in the same way as in their forties and fifties. To claim a signature was a forgery because it was too well written is a joke. Our Bank did everything required or expected to protect Jane Bishop. Her children are doing the opposite. We were not negligent in the slightest and I am proud of our efforts to protect Jane Bishop."

"Your witness for cross examination, Mr. Brown," George said.

Cross Examination

Harold stood and asked** the court for a recess since it was almost 12 noon. The Judge agreed and stated the court would reconvene at 1 p.m. sharp. Harold waited until Henderson had left the courtroom and the police chief had come in before he and Alice and the chief joined Ben in the attorney's room.

Ben addressed the chief, "As soon as Dex returns to court, you need to serve the search warrants and search for the gun and that bottle of Abrin I know he kept. He won't have seen this coming in his arrogance, and I don't think the gun and Abrin will be hidden. Either way, we need that evidence, and I am going to act as though we have it. He may have disposed of the rifle, so I won't make a big thing of it but finding the Abrin is the key."

The chief agreed and assured them, "The warrants will be executed the moment Dex walks back into the court-room." Ben made sure Alice knew how proud of her he was for her handling of Dex without tipping him off to what was coming before Harold and Alice returned to the court-room. When the recess ended, Judge Hacket gaveled the court into session. "You may proceed," he told Harold.

Harold stood to make the statement he had looked forward to for the last ten days. "Your honor, we are now at a point in the trial that my co-counsel Ben Bradshaw had looked forward to. His intention was to cross-examine Mr. Henderson, now in the witness chair, but it was believed he was struck down by an assassin's bullet a week before trial. There has been no motive determined for that vicious assault, but he had come up with a theory that provides an explanation for all of the attacks on him. Armed by that theory, Ben wore a Kevlar, bulletproof vest for the last several months before this trial and I am pleased as I am sure you are all pleased that he is alive and here. He allowed the news of his supposed death to remain public for safety purposes, having been attacked twice with bullets intended to kill him. I turn this cross examination over to my esteemed co-counsel Ben Bradshaw."

It was an extraordinary moment and the courtroom rose and applauded loudly as Ben walked out of the attorney's room and approached Dex Henderson, sitting stunned in the witness chair. Judge Hacket gaveled the courtroom into quiet and told the spectators how great it was to find Ben Bradshaw was alive, but he demanded decorum. "You may proceed, Mr. Bradshaw."

"Hello Dex, my old friend, I have looked forward to seeing you and exchanging words. Are you surprised to see me?"

Almost stuttering as he started to speak, Dex finally said, "Of course, we all thought you were dead."

"I expected you would be surprised since you are the one who shot me, aren't you?" The gasp in the courtroom was audible and it included Judge Hacket's reaction. George would ordinarily object, hoping to keep this attack out of the record but having heard the damning testimony about Dex, he had decided to let the case come in without objection. He already knew he had lost, and the full record would support his work being stymied by the criminal activities of Dex. Trying to shore him up would anger the jury and increase the final verdict.

"That is absurd and false," Dex replied. "You have no basis for such a wild claim, and I intend to sue you for defamation."

"Suing me would be a joke from your prison cell. Let me fill you in on how I know it was you. The police examined the spot on that little hill facing my home where the shooter lay in the undergrowth. They found the casing from the rifle round so they knew they had the precise spot where the potential killer made the shot. They also found several recent drops of blood and were able to match its DNA with guess whose. Yours, Dex. It was you who lay in the brambles and weeds to kill me. I will bet the brambles got you. Is that a band-aid I see on your left hand?"

Dex was literally speechless for several minutes and then continued his arrogant bluster. "That's not true and you know it. This is a frame up to win money for your wife and you won't get away with it."

Ben smiled broadly at Dex's wild claim and continued. "We will leave that fantasy for a moment although you must know we will be back soon enough. You testified there was a green folder containing correspondence between Jane and the Ohio Company. As President of the Bank, it is obvious that you would understand copies of the contents of such a folder would be a necessary part of her mortgage file at the Bank since you pitched the loan committee on granting the loan based on her building homes for her children. Copying the contents would be standard practice for a Bank representative and no one with any brains whatever would assume that folder, if it exists, could be hidden.

The fact is, that if it exists in her belongings, it must have been planted there by you to support your obvious perjury regarding her supposed ability to talk only with you. Jane never prepared a folder of any color, did she?"

"I didn't need to copy anything. My word was sufficient for the loan committee to approve the mortgage. I had seen enough to know she was mentally sound, and her plans were feasible."

"So much for your planted green folder. I want to go way back to Jimmy and Alice's wedding. I remember you admitting being almost overcome with your admiration of Alice and the fact that, as the reception moved along, you appeared more and more morose and left early. You made the crazy decision that Alice should be with you and not with poor Jimmy, didn't you?"

"That's ridiculous. She was married and I congratulated Jimmy on his bride."

"But that's not all you did, was it? You planned a way to get her to see you as her savior, and actually believed she would come to you and love you if given the chance, didn't you?"

"This is so incredibly ridiculous. I should not have to answer but I will. No, is my answer. You are crazy to suggest that."

"Your plan called for killing Jimmy and destroying Alice's finances so that she would have to lean on you, her benefactor, for financial support, leading to her falling for you, didn't it?"

"Again no. This is nonsense. You are the crazy one."

"Stealing Jane's land through foreclosure of her mortgage would give the Bank ownership of a magnificent parcel of land for development. Since Jimmy was a leading developer, your plan was to propose a sale at a bargain price with a promise to back him with the money to develop a subdivision on Jane's seventy-five acres. To make it even more attractive, you personally guaranteed they would not lose their home regardless of any problem that might develop, didn't you?"

"Ho hum, when will this tedious collection of delusions end? No, and again, no. Delusional suggestions are your forte."

"You forget that Alice was there when you made the guarantees to Jimmy and her. She has testified under oath that you demanded inclusion of their home in the collateral for their mortgage and guaranteed the Bank would never take their home. You would see to that personally. That is true, isn't it?"

"Sadly, it is true that I guaranteed their home would be protected, although required as part of their collateral for the loan. I explained to her that the main office had changed the rules so that I could not honor my guarantee despite how much I wanted to help her. I believed it was a matter of honor for me since I had made a guarantee I could not meet."

"But your Vice President, Mary Dobbins, testified that the main Bank's policies have not changed during the past three or four years. You lied to Alice about the supposed change in policy by the main Bank to support your pretense of grief over the alleged change, and that there was nothing you could do about it, didn't you?" Ben demanded.

"That is totally false." Dex was noticeably louder and irritated by this reference and a little sweat formed on his brow that he emphasized when he brushed it away with his sleeve as he answered.

Ben followed. "You thought you had her pinned down at that point, didn't you? While you managed to fake your tears, you were relishing the fact that your plan was working perfectly. Alice was losing her home and all her substantial property through foreclosure, and you were available to hold and comfort her. But a new problem reared its head. Alice and I were working together on a daily basis and to your surprise, we married. Now there was another man in the way to Alice's heart. You hired the killer who had killed Jimmy to kill me for the same reason, to clear the field of anyone Alice might rely on, didn't you?"

"Absolutely not." He was beginning to squirm a little in his seat and the jury was leaning forward on the edge of their seats, intently watching him.

"It is the Plaintiffs' contention that you killed Jane Bishop and Jimmy Jones. That you attempted on two occasions to kill me. How do you answer the Plaintiffs' charge?" Ben pressed him.

Dex was openly sweating now and angrily answered, "You have crossed all boundaries and, in your ignorance and stupidity, have opened yourself to defamation charges which I will bring after this ridiculous case has been dismissed and disposed of by this honest jury."

Ben didn't look but was sure the jury was hanging on every word. He had opened an entirely new area with his claim of murders and the courtroom had become deathly silent during his cross examination. Ben had him set up for the hitman's dying statement and it was time. He addressed the court:

"Your honor, considering the importance of this witness's testimony regarding murders, I wish to offer the Plaintiff's exhibit four into evidence. It is a memorandum of the dying declaration of the man who attempted to kill me in my home two weeks ago. Mr. Brown is furnishing a copy of it to Mr. Faltner with one for Mr. Henderson, as we speak. I will delay further cross examination until Mr. Jeff Barnes has testified to the accuracy of the proposed exhibit."

George made no objection, but Dex objected strongly. The Court had no difficulty denying his objection and allowed the taking of testimony to authenticate the proposed exhibit. Jeff Barnes was brought into the courtroom and took the stand as Dex walked to his chair at the defense counsel's table and visibly enraged, snatched his exhibit copy from George.

Ben started. "Jeff, I have a copy of the memorandum, Plaintiffs' proposed exhibit four, that you made of the assassin's words who attempted to kill me in my home. You are my neighbor and came when you heard gun shots, is that correct?"

"Yes, I came to your front door when the man sent to kill you had just fallen outside the door. His wounds were obvious in his chest and side, and he was bleeding heavily. You and Alice had just kneeled beside him, and I knelt there too as he began speaking. He said he knew he was dying and wanted to tell us why he was there. A few moments after he died, I walked back to my house and wrote down what he said. I believe the document you have in your hand is an accurate presentation of all his words."

Ben handed the memorandum to him and asked Judge Hacket if it would be proper at this point, after Mr. Barnes' testimony, to have him read to the jury and the court the content of Plaintiffs' exhibit four?" Judge Hacket overruled Dex's loud objection and said, "Mr. Barnes can read the exhibit."

Jeff began. "This is what he said, including my description of his condition as he attempted to talk. He began with, "'It's bad, isn't it?' and Ben said, 'Yes." The man continued, 'I am feeling weak, and I know I am dying. I don't blame you, Ranger.' He began coughing and his voice got lower, although I could still hear his words and understand them.

"He went on, 'It was going to happen someday. I was hired by the banker Dex Henderson to kill you and Jimmy Jones. I stopped Jones on the road and knocked him out before sending him over the edge. That arrogant asshole Dex bragged he had poisoned a woman named Jane with Abrin to get her land after stealing a hundred fifty thousand from her. He was so proud of himself, he told me how he had stolen the Abrin and kept the rest of it in case he needed to take care of someone else the same way.'

"His speech was more and more wavering, growing weaker by the moment and his last words before he died were, 'Kill him.'"

The jury was in the throes of such deep anger, Dex Henderson would have been torn limb from limb if he got too close.

"Your witness," Ben said.

George was in total shock at his table, knowing his case had changed from being lost to a certain major verdict. He was through objecting. "To hell with Dex, now exposed as a murderer," George thought. He thought of the discussion with Bank President Henderson giving Dex complete control of the case, and how surprised the father was going to be when he learned his son had been not only a criminal scammer but a murderer. Whatever reaction from the Bank he faced from his decision to stop objecting would be covered by Dex's approval by the Bank's leadership to handle the case so long as he was confident of the result. Dex had continued to express his confidence and George, as the attorney who knew now he was going to lose a huge verdict against the Bank, took comfort from the fact the Bank's President had dictated his actions.

Dex was shaking with anger at what that son of a bitch Ray had done. He tried to figure out why since he had believed they had a good working relationship but his delusional belief in his superiority made him incapable of understanding how his arrogance had fostered Ray's contempt. He knew it was too late to object or attempt cross examination and stated he had no questions. He knew now what he had to do.

George stated, "I have no questions."

Ben then said, "I call Alice Bradshaw to the stand." Alice stood and walked to the witness box to be sworn.

"Alice, were you there when that man shot me, and did you hear what that he said as he lay dying?"

"Yes, I was in the kitchen when I heard the doorbell and walked into the hall just as you opened the door. I heard gunshots as you fell to the ground. I screamed and ran to fall and cover you, but you had already fired two shots and he was falling onto the sidewalk outside our door. You held me for a few moments and then helped me to my feet, telling me you were all right, not to worry. We walked out to the man who had shot you, and he was terribly wounded with blood coming from his chest and side in a steady stream. I could see there was nothing we could do for him, and we kneeled beside him as he talked. I have read the memo Jeff prepared and it is a completely accurate record of what that hired killer said.

"When he told us Dex Henderson was behind the attack on you and about Jimmy and Jane's murders, I remember such a sense of rage I could hardly keep from screaming. When he said Henderson had ordered Jimmy's killing and had poisoned Jane, all I wanted was for him to be jailed for the rest of his life."

Ben said, "Your witness."

George and Dex again said they had no questions. By this time Dex was growing grimmer by the minute. Even he could see the handwriting on the wall and knew he was in entirely unforeseen trouble with a capital T. He knew his problem was Ben. He realized he had underestimated Ben's intelligence and it had bitten him. All he could think about was getting back at Ben and taking charge of this fiasco.

Ben turned and said, "I call Mr. Henderson to the stand for continuation of my cross examination." Dex walked leisurely to the stand and smiled at Ben as he passed him. Ben was deeply concerned by that smile and apparent willingness to testify. He had been worried about the potential ability of Dex to secrete a gun on his person and had been keeping his right hand as close as possible to the grip of his Glock, well-hidden but ready.

As Dex climbed into the witness box with his back to Ben, he drew his hidden gun from behind that large metal belt buckle and turned with it pointed at Ben. It was so quick there was no chance for Ben to draw. Dex called out in a loud voice, "If anyone in the room moves, I will immediately kill Ben and that bitch he married. I am in charge, and you all had better understand that or there will be a lot of deaths. I have the only gun in the room and intend to use it. This is an automatic with a full clip, so, just settle down while I tell you the real score. You are all so dumb I have been screwing you for your money for years and when I walk out that door you will never find me or see me again.

"All of you, look at the mighty Ranger standing helpless in front of me. What a fool he is. He thinks he can save himself and his whore wife with his fancy shooting. But who has the only gun now? It's a laugh. And how about his wife, the whore who marries over and over to whatever man can support her. She didn't have the brains to know I am the only real man she ever needed. Her obvious stupidity caused her to miss the boat and she is going to die with her current fool of a husband.

"I am in charge, not this fool of a poor, shaking attorney standing in front of you. Yes, I killed Jane to get her land and hired the man who killed Jimmy and tried to kill this puny, insignificant attorney that I put a bullet into to finish the job. He lucked out with his Kevlar vest, but his luck has run out. I intend to finish the job and kill his bitch wife along with him. I will also kill anyone who tries to help these two before I shoot them. I will then walk out of court keeping you all under my gun. I may shoot a few of you for fun, or I may not. Depends on how quiet you stay and if no one moves as I disappear into thin air like a ghost. I have the money required to disappear and a perfect plan to make it happen. After leaving this courtroom, I will wait outside so that I can shoot the first ones who come through the door. Believe me when I say that I won't miss and will enjoy killing anyone who tries to leave."

During this incredible spiel Ben was standing quietly in front of him, confident that Alice was just a little behind in what he assumed was a straight line. He kept his eyes looking slightly downward knowing that direct eye contact with Dex would potentially trigger the shooting of himself and Alice without much of a chance to stop it. He knew if he moved to the right while drawing the Glock, he would put Harold and the Plaintiffs' counsel table in the line of fire whereas a movement left would move Dex's line of fire toward the almost empty Defendants' table. The more people he removed from Dex's shooting lane the better, he thought. He knew he had to move in order to force Dex to move his shots away from Alice to counter Ben's movement. His priority was saving Alice, and he was ready to die to do so. He thought he would know when Dex was about to pull the trigger and watched him intently without looking into his eyes. All he needed he thought was a moment where Dex lost focus and Ben's sudden movement to his left would cause Dex's aim to shift to follow him. It was his only chance to beat Dex to the first shot and slim at best. He knew the police in the crowd of spectators would jump into the fire fight and finish Dex if he was unsuccessful.

Meantime, Dex continued to rant. "You will never understand anything that I do or have done. I have done nothing but fulfil my destiny. My mind has capabilities so far beyond your limited comprehension that these puny efforts to beat me in a court case are a joke. I am sure you, the jury, will screw the Bank royally and I don't give a damn how much you give these asinine Plaintiffs. It won't mean a thing to these two quaking idiots in front of me who will never see a dime of it. Your idiot Chief of Police would never have known any of this except for the lucky words from Ray, my hitman who finished off Jimmy but failed with this quavering attorney standing in front of me who will never see another day, with or without his bitch wife. So far as insignificant Jane Bishop, I should get a medal for ending her drain on society and I enjoyed watching her die. She was no loss and my finishing her was simple euthanasia.

"All of you in this courtroom will be treated to the sound of my gun as I finish them off along with the Judge who has consistently approved of their attack on me. My killing gun shots will be the last noise they hear when I dispose of all three of them. Some of you will also hear it in your last moment if you screw up after I finish them. The slightest movement from anyone and this is what you will hear." He lifted his gun high over his head and fired into the ceiling in a blatant show of his power over everyone in the room. The noise of the shot was devastating, and he was gratified by the absolute stillness and silence of the room. He was in control and loving every moment of what he perceived as total power along with everyone's obvious fear of him.

His momentary lack of focus as he raised his gun to fire into the ceiling gave Ben the chance he had waited for without much hope. His reflexes, honed over years in combat, took over and his Glock appeared in his hand in an instant in what was probably the fastest draw of his life. His earlier plan to throw himself sideways to disrupt Dex's aim while drawing it away from Alice was gone in a flash. Dex was just bringing his gun back down to shoot Ben and Alice when Ben's two rapid shots hit him in his heart. Dex was dying as he crumpled and fell forward from the witness box. The inexorable pull of gravity on the weight of his gun caused his finger to pull the trigger and his bullet went into the floor only inches from Ben's feet. The shocked look of surprise on Dex's face was his last function as he fell from the witness box to the floor of the courtroom, his blood pouring onto Ben's shoes. Alice screamed, leaped forward grabbing for Ben and collapsed almost headfirst to the floor and into the blood, believing that Dex's shot had hit him.

The gunshots had been so sudden the jury and courtroom observers were stunned. Several women screamed hysterically at the scene of Alice collapsed at Ben's feet in Dex's pooling blood. It was terrible to see and most of the women in the audience turned away in horror. There was a cumulative gasp from the courtroom as Ben raised her to her feet, bloody and in shock. Someone began clapping and there was sudden, deafening clapping and cheering from everyone in the courtroom.

It was an incredible ending to Dex's vicious threats to all of them. They had been held under his gun and had watched him unmasked as a serial killer by his confession of multiple murders. His death from Ben's gunshots was so sudden and unexpected it seemed unbelievable. There was a palpable sense of relief in the room joined with universal admiration for Ben and Alice.

The undercover police in the courtroom had leaped forward, guns in hand to meet Dex's response, if any, to Ben's shots. They had waited for the chance that Ben had taken advantage of, certain that a shootout with Dex would lead to multiple deaths in the room. With Dex's body on the floor and the danger passed, they took Ben's gun without any complaint from him.

Ben's first thought was that Alice's terror for him was finally over and he stood quietly in front of the Judge's bench. He had lifted Alice up and she was clinging to him in what amounted to a desperate hug. Ben's lightning reflexes and Alice's love for him were a combination that would become legend in the city. He held her close, returning her strong hug, turning finally to sit at the Plaintiffs' counsel table with her, Harold, and the Bishops. They were holding each other and weeping at the disclosure that their mother had been murdered and died in pain while her murderer enjoyed her agony.

Alice was still in shock, with blood staining her clothes and marking her face and hands. She was still holding Ben with a grip he made no attempt to loosen. He held her close as she trembled, telling her over and over it was all right, he was all right and Dex was no longer a threat to them. She gradually calmed down and relaxed her initial death grip. He left the cleanup of the courtroom and legal issues with Harold and rushed her into their car.

They arrived home to a hero's welcome from Joe and Jeff. Ben gave them the full story while she headed to the shower.

The Chief of police came by shortly with the State Police Sergeant and the results of the search warrants. The rifle had been in the trunk of Dex's car and the Abrin was in his medicine cabinet. They had also found his files which included copies of his DBA in Ohio and several sheets on which he had practiced Jane's signature. It was apparent he had no worry about anyone ever figuring him out. His erotic notes on what he would be doing with Alice were so graphic and ugly Ben disposed of them immediately. They confirmed Ben's idea of the motive but, with Dex's death, were no longer needed.

The police Chief thanked Ben for his identification and finally, in self-defense, killing of a serial killer who would have continued killing. "I confess," he said, "that I was very uneasy letting Henderson take part in the trial without arresting him up front, but you carried it off just as you and Joe promised."

After the police left and Joe and Jeff had headed out the door, Ben and Alice were together alone for the first time in days. He had intended going over his final argument but said, "I have something else in mind." He locked the doors and met her in the bedroom. "It beats a final argument," he thought, and she must have agreed because they were there for a long time and there were no arguments. She consigned her bloodied clothing to the trash. A final and appropriate goodbye to the ugly killer who had attacked them.

Judge Hacket, more than a little unraveled from his deep concern about the threats of multiple deaths including his own, and dealing with removal of Dex's body, had told Harold and George that court would reopen the next day at 9 a.m. That evening, Ben and Harold talked on the phone, and both thought the jury was ready to teach the Bank a very painful lesson. The failure to recognize the continued strong signatures as forgeries was particularly negligent conduct and should have raised serious questions about his contacts with her. The arguments to the jury would emphasize the Bank's having total knowledge because Dex had known everything as an employee of the Bank.

They agreed that Harold should begin the final argument with the Bishops' case and that Ben would follow and finish with Alice's case. After Ben and Alice had left the courtroom, Harold had joined George in Judge Hacket's office and agreed they would rest the Plaintiffs' case and make their final arguments in the morning. George indicated he did not intend to call additional witnesses and would also rest the Defendant's case. It appeared that, after final arguments and the Judge's charges to the jury, it would begin its deliberations by the afternoon.

At nine a.m. the following day, all parties were in the courtroom ready to begin final arguments. The Judge gaveled the court into session; the Plaintiffs rested their case; and George, in a state of despair, rested the defense case. He had no rebuttal and knew it.

Final Arguments

Harold stood, walked to the lectern in front of the jury, and began his final argument.

"Ladies and gentlemen of the jury, I am going to be brief because this has been one of the most incredible trials I have ever participated in and, I suspect, is a trial you will tell your children and friends about for years. I want to say how great it has been to stand alongside Ben Bradshaw, the finest attorney I have ever known. After three deliberate attempts on his life, he stands as a proud Army Ranger who has fought for our country and then to protect his wife, you the jury and entire courtroom of spectators against the assault of a determined enemy who had been hiding behind the guise of friendship. Who among us would have had the brains and strength to name and finally kill in self-defense the President of our local Bank who posed as a good fellow while engaging in serial killing?

"We found evidence of Henderson's scams. We showed you in chapter and verse, how he forged the mortgage and checks of Jane Bishop to steal a total of more than one hundred fifty thousand dollars from her bank account and then her property valued at three million dollars. That wasn't enough for that cold blooded killer. He poisoned a ninety-three-year-old woman and watched her die in pain, coughing her life away. It doesn't matter that she had lost her cognitive faculties, she was a wonderful, loving mother who had been a leader in our community and deserved to meet her maker on her terms surrounded by her children who loved her, not on a brutal killer's terms.

"We have proved the compensatory damages to the Bishops. The gross negligence of the Bank that has been demonstrated by so much cumulative testimony requires more. The Bank's vice president, Mary Dobbins said it best. The Bank needs to make it right. The Bank needs to pay punitive damages for the anguish of this family directly caused by the Bank's failure to protect her and its gross negligence in failing to see the criminal activities of its President over a period of years. The Defendant Bank knew everything its local president, as an employee of the Bank, knew, regardless of his criminal activities. The Bank needs to be told with punitive damages that what it did to 93-year-old Jane Bishop, was wrong and to never do anything like it again. It must be told in no uncertain terms that it must change its business model to do what it claimed was its policy to protect seniors. You have seen that it grossly failed to protect Jane Bishop.

"On behalf of my clients, John Bishop, David Bishop and Sylvia Bishop Turner, I ask that you award them four and one half million in compensatory damages and a minimum of five million in punitive damages to send the necessary message that what the Bank did was wrong and must stop. It is impossible to just return their property in the condition it was at the time of her death. It has been completely developed as a subdivision and the home she and they loved no longer exists. The only winner so far has been the Bank that earned a million dollars on the foreclosure while demolishing Jane Bishop's estate and stealing her property worth three million dollars with its sham foreclosure. The Defendant Bank then planned to steal another eight million dollars from Alice Bradshaw. There seems no limit to the Bank's greed.

"I want to again make the most important argument we believe supports the verdict we ask you to render. Dex Henderson was a serial killer while serving the Defendant Bank as President of its local branch. He represented the Bank in all matters involving Jane Bishop and Alice Bradshaw. The Defendant Bank is responsible for the actions of its employee and the Defendant Bank legally knew what he knew from the beginning. That is regardless of his criminal actions. His criminality is not a defense the Bank can use to claim no knowledge of the multiple frauds so as to defeat the claims of the Plaintiffs.

"I thank you for your attention and believe we have given you the true facts that overpower any opposition to my summation. I have just one simple request. I ask you to do what the Defendant's local branch Vice President, Mary Dobbins, wanted to do. She hit a home run based on her honesty and compassion with her heartfelt statement. She said, 'Make it right.'"

He sat down and Ben stepped in front of the jury to make the final argument on behalf of Alice.

"This case should not be about my service as an Army Ranger and the fact that I was forced to defend Alice and the rest of us. All of that is irrelevant but, it is relevant that I am the luckiest man on earth because I am married to her and have this opportunity to discuss with you her resolve, her strength and her brilliance in fighting against the Bank and its brutal, murdering branch president who formed his evil plan to claim her for his own. Representing the Defendant Bank, he attempted to destroy her financial security as a path to forcing himself upon her. You have heard the testimony demonstrating her battle with him and his Bank. She never wavered and she has given me her strength to ask you to finish the ugly, murderous war he began. She asks that your verdict tells him and his Bank they have lost that war.

"I hope you will never see another trial with the drama and ultimate danger of this one. I am hopeful there will never be another morally bankrupt, obsession driven murderer like Dex Henderson to blacken the reputation of our marvelous community.

"I really liked Jimmy Jones. He became my best friend in Traverse City and made my move from Detroit exceptionally pleasant. His death was a tremendous loss for all of us who knew him. He was a skilled developer dedicated to building beautiful subdivisions that stood out for their quality and livability. He and Alice were deeply in love and his loss so soon in their marriage was a terrible blow to her, causing a long period of anguish and serious questions about why and how he had died.

"She concluded Jimmy's accident was phony and that he was murdered. When she described the circumstances of his crash, I believed she was right. We decided to wear protection in the form of a Kevlar vest since there was no reason to believe she was also not in danger. She learned to shoot her pistol and we both carried them from that point forward. Fortunately, my vest stopped Henderson's killer's bullets. When I returned fire and he was fatally wounded, we heard his dying declaration and knew, for the first time, who our enemy was.

"We began a deep investigation and our investigator found much of the evidence Harold presented to you including the handwriting expert who proved with his testimony that Henderson had been forging Jane's signature for more than a year and had stripped one hundred fifty thousand from her account before his master stroke with his forged mortgage.

"The Bank never had good title to the land it sold Jimmy and Alice and the additional funds for a total of five million dollars were clearly intended to put Jimmy and Alice in debt so large they could not meet the Bank's call before the subdivision was completed. I have no doubt that Dex intended the demand for their payment would come before lot sales could begin. Think about the deliberate, fraudulent and shameful call Dex and the Defendant Bank made on Jimmy and Alice's mortgage only thirty days after Jimmy's death. They were less than three months away from the lot sales that would yield magnificent profits. Henderson knew the mortgage call would be impossible to meet. He engineered a deliberate, criminal theft of the legitimate profits that would have flowed from sales of lots in the premier subdivision, almost completed. It was an evil plan carried out with perfection.

"Dex made sure the Bank had taken Jane Bishop's land, valued at three million dollars after an investment of only nine hundred thousand dollars. A sale of Alice's subdivision by the Bank after foreclosing on her would give the Bank land worth at least twelve million dollars with only four million invested. The Bank stood to make close to eight million dollars over and above its investment. Dex stood to be praised and bonused by his superiors in the Defendant Bank while accomplishing his marvelous plan to destroy Jimmy and Alice's finances.

"Her loss is the eight-million-dollar loss from sales and the five million paid the Bank and contractors for the purchase and development of the land. All based on a false, forged mortgage foreclosed against Jane Bishop. The Bank cannot claim ownership of the money it used to scam her, and Alice has the right to claim the full amount of the lost profit from sales, the full eight million and the five million spent to build her subdivision, some of which is owed the Bank for property criminally sold her without good title with the balance having been committed to contractors working on a subdivision built on land fraudulently sold to Jimmy and her. She cannot finish the subdivision and it goes down the drain since she can claim no ownership interest.

"So, who should take the loss from a fraudulent sale? I say the Defendant Bank should, not Alice who it defrauded.

"I want to point out that the Bank received almost two million dollars from its foreclosure of Jane's property as a return on its nine-hundred-thousand-dollar mortgage when it sold her land to Jimmy for just under two million dollars. The Bank doubled its money on the deal. Not too bad for a Bank so negligent it allowed its President to score one hundred fifty thousand from a depositor's account while taking another million and a half on the deal. Let's not cry for the Bank and its crocodile tears. It is rolling in its money from Jane Bishop's criminally based foreclosure and its potential, huge profits from its foreclosure of Alice's property, including her home.

"This is a good place for me to say that Harold is way too much of a gentleman. He asks for punitive damages of a minimum five million dollars when you should be considering double that amount for the Bishop children who have been vilified by the defense as greedy. Talk about irony. It is the Bank that is greedy in this case. This Bank can laugh all the way to its Board of Directors if you find only picayune punitive damages. The lesson must be severe, or it will mean nothing.

"I am in a strange, unusual position as her husband arguing for damages for Alice. I would not be here except that I have more knowledge of her periods of deep grief over the death of Jimmy and what she has gone through as I have been relentlessly attacked. She and Jimmy were close to completion of their superb subdivision on Jane's land when Jimmy was murdered. He was murdered to ensure she would be financially destitute and a supposed willing target for Henderson's lust. Alice testified they owed about five million on what amounted to a sham mortgage when Jimmy was killed and were within three months of potential sales that would have netted them profits of a minimum of eight million dollars over and above their mortgage. All that disappeared when Henderson pulled the plug on their mortgage and began foreclosure within thirty days of his death. We have stopped that foreclosure with this case since the title to the land the Bank sold them is no good, but that is not enough.

"We have shown the gross negligence of the Defendant Bank, and that Alice deserves the chance to save her reputation in the community. Unfortunately, it is my opinion that folks have had a strong tendency for years to believe Banks are usually honest and to blame the people whose property is foreclosed for inability to pay a debt they incurred. I have observed what she has gone through and have lived with her pain. It cannot be forgotten with words such as 'sorry' or 'I always knew you were right.' She has been savaged by the Bank. Henderson was its representative and spoke for the Bank. The Bank cannot say it doesn't know him or that he didn't have the authority to act for the Bank. The important fact to remember is that the Bank knew everything its President knew as a matter of law.

I want you to think about what Alice has gone through

in the last two years. She lost her loving husband, Jimmy. She grieved for half a year and then, after we were married, watched me shot in front of her, thinking I was also dead. That was not enough. With about a week until this trial, she sat on our patio with me and watched me being blown backward by a rifle bullet to my heart. Then, as you all saw, she saw Henderson hold a gun on me and state he intended to kill us both there in the courtroom. She testified she was still scared before that happened and lived through another session of terror. I took her home to wash his blood off her body and hold her long and hard in an attempt to ease her pain and terror. It will be impossible to get that awful scene from her mind. She will live with it for the rest of her life. The law provides only money for damages so that is her only remedy for the inconceivable trauma.

"So, I ask that you award her the five million she and Jimmy spent on the untitled land fraudulently sold to them by the Defendant Bank and the eight million in profits from their gorgeous subdivision lost because of the Bank's fraud. She cannot proceed with her subdivision since she no longer owns the land because the Bank's foreclosure of Jane Bishop's land was illegally based on a forged mortgage. Her compensatory damages are her lost profit of eight million and the five million paid the Bank and contractors on the subdivision. Remember that the Defendant Bank took her mortgage for five million dollars while knowing what its President knew; that the title of the land was bad and that the Bank would be taking over the entire project. For an investment of less than three million it would have received eight million or more. The Defendant Bank's win would have been the total of her compensatory damages of thirteen million dollars.

Finally, I ask that you award punitive damages for what the Bank put her through and make sure they don't do it to someone else in the future. I believe that, when you consider what the Bank did to her, you will find a figure to make sure they don't do it to someone else. I ask that you award Alice a minimum of fifteen million dollars in punitive damages and thirteen million dollars in compensatory damages. Anything less in punitive damages will hardly faze the Defendant Bank's board of directors. Remember the Bank mortgaged land it sold with a false title and supported the false title with a false mortgage while knowing all the time the mortgage was forged. I say again, the Bank is charged with the knowledge of its President despite his criminal actions. Do what Mary Robbins said. Make it right.

"Thank you for your attention."

George apologized for the Bank's actions and conceded that the Plaintiffs were entitled to relief. He asked the jury to be reasonable and not to be too affected by the drama in court and the criminal actions of just one employee of the Bank.

Judge Hacket's charges were precise and thorough. George agreed with Ben and Harold the charges had been appropriate and the Judge turned the jury over to the bailiff.

Verdict

It had only been an hour before the bailiff told the Judge the jury had a verdict. Judge Hacket called all parties into court and directed the bailiff to bring the jury in. When they had taken their seats, he asked whether they had elected a foreman and one of the ladies raised her hand. "I am foreperson," she said. The Judge asked if the jury had reached a verdict and she said, "Yes, we have." Judge Hacket directed her to hand the verdict form to the bailiff who brought it to the Judge. He had it returned to the foreperson and directed her to read it. She stood and turned to look at the Plaintiffs and began.

"We, the jury find for Plaintiffs Bishop as follows: We set aside the foreclosure on Jane Bishop's property and return it to her estate. In addition, we award the sum of three million dollars to the estate of Jane Bishop as compensatory damages. In determining compensatory damages, we considered the property has value although no appraisal was offered. We further award them the sum of nine million dollars in punitive damages against the Defendant Bank."

She continued, "We the jury find for Plaintiff Alice Bradshaw against the Defendant Bank and award her the sum of thirteen million dollars in compensatory damages, and punitive damages in the amount of ten million dollars against the Defendant Bank."

Judge Hacket asked the individual members of the jury if they agreed with the verdict and each one stated loudly and positively, yes.

The Plaintiffs were in shock and overwhelmed at what Harold and Ben had accomplished. There were tears and handshakes around the table and the Bishops found themselves totally proven right about their fighting mother. We did it, they said and embraced warmly. Ben proposed meeting for dinner for a celebration and it was received with acclaim by all. He continued, "I think a verdict of this size would be automatically appealed but, under the circumstances of Henderson's criminal, murderous actions and his father being President of the Bank, I don't imagine there will be any stomach for further litigation. It's interesting that daddy left the trial up to his son and I think it proves he had no idea what a morally bankrupt child he had. The last thing the Bank will want is more publicity and an appeal would ensure just that. I will be amazed if they appeal. They can more easily take a thirty-five-million-dollar verdict than widespread public recognition of the Bank's failure to recognize it had a serial murderer and scammer as President of its branch. Continued discussion of its fraudulent actions against a ninety-three-year-old victim would be ugly public relations, damaging as hell to them. What do you think, Harold?"

Harold agreed and was just as confident there would be no appeal. "I don't think they will want the knowledge of the Bank's branch president being killed while attempting to murder the Plaintiff's counsel, to go viral. We owe this all to you, Ben. You choreographed the trial, fought off his assassin and defended us all against Dex with your bravery. I am proud to have been associated with you in this trial."

Ben took him aside and said, "I would like us to join as partners if you think it is something you would enjoy." Harold answered, "It is something that I would like very much. I can think of nothing better than working with you."

Ben's answer was indicative of his great pleasure. "You handled the trial with superb lawyering. It will be Alice's and my great gain to join you and Angie in the newest firm in Traverse City, Brown and Bradshaw." They announced the agreement to the group and were met with congratulations all around.

The celebratory meal at the excellent, downtown restaurant, Modes, was exceptional and there could be no happier group anywhere that evening. Ben and Alice arrived home for a night of lovemaking that seemed a long-delayed extension of yesterday's loving. He jokingly asked if she was going to stay with him now that she owned the world. She flamed in anger at his remark. "I won't ever let you joke about us," she said. "I never will again," he promised sheepishly, loving her intensity.

Finish

Harold and Ben worked out an agreement for Alice and the Bishops. Alice would finish the subdivision and handle sales for a split of the profits, a terrific result for everyone. The need for a larger office space for the partnership was satisfied when Ben found a new listing for a large home zoned for office use and located only a few blocks from downtown.

The meeting of Ben and Alice's families that had been delayed during the trial preparation, finally came. It was obvious they were made for each other and when Ben and Alice announced that Alice was expecting, it was sensational news and a fitting climax to what had already been several days of celebration.

Home after the family love fest, they sat in their kitchen with cups of coffee and reminisced. He summed it up with, "Can't imagine a better few days but it seems that you are sad or troubled. What's up? Anything I have done or can do?"

Her answer was difficult for her. "My mind is telling me that I should be the happiest woman in the world with you by my side, the man I love more than life itself. But I can't seem to shake the underlying fear that someone is going to come at us like what we just went through. I know I should be able to dismiss it as fantasy but it's there in my mind and it stays there no matter how certain I am that we are past such concerns. I will be going along so happy about the child coming and suddenly be holding back a scream as I see a picture of you, lying on the floor in a pool of blood. I hate to admit how scared I was and how that fear comes back with each vivid picture.

"I have decided to carry my Glock for so long as I am battling those ugly, frightening times, and I want to practice with it until I am expert enough to know that I can defend our family. I know I will never equal your ability but want to be the second best shot in town. I like shooting and believe I can become better than just good at it. We can call it a hobby or whatever, but I want us to be on the range often enough for me to achieve the ability to protect us. I don't want our children to have a mother scared all the time and am confident this will help my scary visions to pass sooner rather than later. When they stop the Glock will be locked away rather than in perpetual practice and meantime, you will continue to have the most passionate wife any man has ever encountered. So, just hold me often and keep on loving me as you are each day. This will all be forgotten soon enough."

Ben took her in his arms. "Your concern is understandable. A weaker woman would have cracked wide open long before now and your strength has helped me face the madness. I am confident you will get through this, no matter how long it takes."

He looked into those incredible green eyes and made her a promise. "I will stick so close to you until you have this licked that you will think of me as a burr on your skin. I will buy a thin, underarm holster to make carrying your Glock easier and even less conspicuous. We will follow through on improving your shooting skills and make this home impregnable to attack. We will replace the windows with bulletproof glass including glass walls around the patio. We'll set up surveillance cameras all around the house and on that little hill where that son of a bitch lay to make his shot. Our cameras will monitor the entire area including the street in front.

Our children will have us both protecting them and if someone tries to challenge us, we will handle him as we did that asshole Dex. We will hire bodyguards for you and our children for as long as we believe necessary. They will be unobtrusive guards you must approve of since safety requires they remain in close proximity at all times. They should be treated like members of the family. I don't know if we can convince Joe to take the job coordinating but will pay him whatever it takes if he will. I know we can depend on him to assist us in setting up the house as a fortress. I also know he has a handle on men and women capable of protecting us and anyone he brings on board will be damned capable and welcomed.

This lot is large enough to permit building a substantial addition to the house. If you think a safe room is advisable, it could be large and comfortable with its own utilities and generator. There are architects who specialize in their design, and we can make sure all eventualities are taken care of.

I think we should build quarters for the staff we hire as well as an indoor exercise pool. When we no longer need protection, their rooms, with a small kitchen, dining area and living room, will be great guest rooms for our families. We will figure it all out together as we always have. I am particularly pleased the verdict against that bastard's bank has paid for whatever we decide to build and the protection we bring on board.

We will make a life our family will enjoy. You have no need to worry whether I will keep on loving and cherishing you. Having you love me makes me the luckiest man ever born and I plan on doing everything in my power for the rest of my life to maintain that status."

Their passionate kiss was a fitting end to an incredible year that had started with Jimmy's murder and ended with love.

THE END

ABOUT THE AUTHOR

Robert Steadman grew up near Syracuse, New York, the second oldest of five children. The family moved to Michigan, where his dad was hired as the state's financial controller. Bob graduated from Wayne University Law School in February of 1951, having earned his Bachelor of Arts, Bachelor of Law, and Juris Doctor degrees in five and a half years, all while working nights on the Ford River Rouge Plant's engine line. Drafted in May of 1951 for the Korean conflict, he completed Officer Candidate School and was discharged as a second lieutenant late in 1953.

Steadman had the good fortune of working one year with the best attorney in Flint and also a year as assistant prosecutor, an intensive introduction to trial work.

While learning to fly at Flint's Bishop Airport, he met and married his instructor, Bernice Trimble, already a famous racing pilot, in 1959. His aviation expertise led to a position as corporate and trial attorney for Airway Insurance Company in Ann Arbor, where he defended aviation death cases from Massachusetts to Alaska for several years. He turned down the company presidency in 1972 and chose to move to Traverse City instead.

Bob was eighty-one in 2009 when he tried and won his last jury trial with an award of $400,000 for his client against a local bank for fraud. He then cared for Bernice during her remaining years of illness, in their home. She passed away in 2015 after fifty-six wonderful years together. From 2018 to 2022 he served as President of Senior Center Friends, an organization he formed with his brother Richard and brilliant, best friend, Lillian Ostendorf, to fight for a new Senior Center in Traverse City. Successful in their advocacy, they look forward to walking into the new Senior Center, currently under construction, in the coming fall. At the young age of ninety-five, he spends his time writing, rooting for the Detroit Lions, Tigers, Red Wings and Pistons, while enjoying his Shorthair Pointer Belle and bridge with his friends.